ZEPHYRIAN SPOOLS
(An Essay, A Wind)
DALIA NEIS

KFS

Newton-le-Willows

Published in the United Kingdom in 2020
by The Knives Forks And Spoons Press,
51 Pipit Avenue,
Newton-le-Willows,
Merseyside,
WA12 9RG.

ISBN 978-1-912211-51-7

Copyright © Dalia Neis, 2020.

The right of Dalia Neis to be identified as the author of this work has been asserted by them in accordance with the Copyrights, Designs and Patents Act of 1988. All rights reserved. No part of this publication may be reproduced, stored in a retrieval system, transmitted in any form or by any means, electronic, photocopying, recording or otherwise, without prior permission of the publisher.

Acknowledgements:

Excerpts from this essay, including 'Nothing of the Human', featured as song lyrics for the track 'Gish' in the self-titled debut album of the music/poetry group FITH, released by Wanda in November 2016. '1928' (from 'The Magic Stone – Winds from the Zone' epilogue), featured as a spoken word/musical performance in FITH's live concerts since 2017 and as an improvised recording, entitled 'Double Exposure', in collaboration with Rachel Margetts on the *Wanda is Not Here* mixtape released by Wanda/Ono records in July 2016. '1928 (The Year of Magical Thinking) – Totality' appeared in the 'Pure Fiction' Magazine in September 2018. A version of '*Silent Cinema's Sublime Winds – The Unfilmable*' and '*Silent Cinema's Sublime Winds – Spinozist Visions*' appeared in *Senses of Cinema's* 'Straub-Huillet' dossier in September 2019. Initially broadcast as a recitation piece for NTS Radio in September 2018, 'Cassiopeia the Queen', and 'Post Vision©' have since evolved into new FITH songs entitled 'Białystok' and 'Swamp', both of which appear in a record released by Outer Reaches in June 2019.

With special thanks to Ursula Hurley for guiding me throughout the writing process, to Rona Lorimer for proof reading and editing an earlier version which appeared in my doctoral thesis, and to Alec Newman for all his input in bringing this out into the world. With deep gratitude to Justin Barton, Scott Thurston, Iwajla Klinke, Andreas Reihse, Tatia Shaburishivili, Iori Wallace, Hannah Berry, Enir Da, and FITH, who blew my inquiries into unforeseen paths.

For Çiğdem

*Nothing of the human remained
As she straddled the southwest frontier*

*Hat blown and windswept
She hovers across the spheres*

*The holy wind devoured her
But it was she that called its name*

*Summoning the outside
For the sake of the sacred game*

Zephyrian Spools (An Essay, A Wind)

Memories of a Northern Wind – Clitoral Visions

My relationship with wind began in early childhood. My life was confined to the ghetto on my street, in which several aunts and uncles, and dozens of cousins and distant relatives lived. At school the playground was a vast field of land that stretched out towards the North Circular. I tried my best to escape several times, and found a hole through the barbed-wired fence that led to an enclosed patch of densely growing weeds and oak trees, which I later discovered was the lingering home to a notorious flasher who zapped open his trench coat upon meeting me in a dark alley. My only other exposures to the outside were occasional rides on the milk float, annual trips to the circus, and weekly visits to the park. My father would take me to Brent Park on the edge of the North Circular, just before the end of the Sabbath. Brent Park oozed a gloomy, dark energy, and would feature in my dreams as a kingdom inhabited by nonhuman entities of various malignant and benign natures. The park felt prehistoric, and I sensed that there were force-fields streaming through the river, and across the three ponds at the park's centre. As I walked through the park's crooked walkways I fell further away from suburban logic and order, and drew deeper into the world of primordial stories and clitoral visions.

At Brent Park, before the end of the Sabbath, my father would push me on the swings high up into the air, and on the way down during those moments of flight, I felt the wind blow into me, which would give me a sense of euphoric freedom. That moment of being up in the air, and circulating within it, however brief, altered my sense of space and time, dilating that instant into a thread of perceptual epiphanies and glimpses into other dimensions. In swinging an almost 360 degrees full circle I would experience myself as a roving, spherical eye, seeing with parts of my body that I would not normally associate with vision. I began to convince myself that while up there, mid-flight, swirling into the wind-blown autumnal leaves, that I had eyes at the back of my head, on the palms of my hands, on the soles of my feet, and on the tip of my clitoris. The air had opened up the pores of my body to an awareness of sight beyond the ocular; a sublime slippage between sight, vision, and eye would play itself out on the tips of my skin and beneath my pores.

The auto-erotic nature of this experience sparked an early curiosity in my grandfather's rumoured breathing techniques which he practised in the forest on long solitary periods during his teens on the outskirts of Białystok, near the border of Belarus. My grandfather came from a long lineage of Chassidic practice known as the 'Breslov Chassidic Movement', originating in the teachings of Rabbi Nachman of Breslev in the Ukraine. This branch of Chassidism flourished in Eastern Europe from the beginning of the eighteenth century. Rabbi Nachman encouraged solitary meditation in nature, and would instruct a non-conformist practice of Judaism, which was less about institutional rules and regulations, and more about forging connections with the material world, involving midnight excursions to forests, meditational breathing techniques, and frenetic circular dancing.

Apart from this pantheistic lineage of Chassidic influence, my grandfather also used to cite the names of seven scholars, all of whom were women, who had purportedly taught him a striking and more secretive form of knowledge: "There was Shoshana the Elder, Tamarah the Talmudist, Devoreleh the Kabbalist, Eleanora the Levitator, Faigle the Wordsmith, Sara the Siren, and Lilit the Seer."

These names and occupations eventually became a secret incantation. I would repeat these names and rare sounding occupations back to myself.

"Shoshana the Elder, Tamarah the Talmudist, Devoreleh the Kabbalist, Eleanora the Levitator, Faigle the Wordsmith, Sara the Siren, and Lilit the Seer."

"Then one day in 1928 they disappeared, just like that!" My grandfather exclaimed and clicked his fingers to emphasise their mysterious and abrupt departure.

"But where did they go?" I asked.

"They went away with the wind. They rode on its back to Prague," he replied, and would refuse to go into any more detail.

My grandfather practised the teachings of these seven scholars, and combined them with a fervent form of Chassidic rapture and communication with his surroundings. He would spend hours talking to birds perched on the trees, and communicated to the wind through breath and movement, combining choreographed dance techniques with guttural breath sounds and nude swimming in ice cold streams. I once asked him to teach me his techniques, to which he replied that he thought that I already knew the language of wind through my swinging experience in the park (I had told him in great detail about my experiences on the swing, carefully omitting my clitoral visions).

Later on, when I began to fall in love with boys and then later, girls, this process often began as a kind of wind-swept, frenzied awe of the way the person's hair blew in the breeze. This dance of air and hair never ceased to enrapture me. I began to believe that the spirit pointed me out to the person whose hair stood out in the wind. This fascination has since continued into other terrains, and into the medium of cinema in particular, in which this gesture is magnified, stretched out and brought to the foreground: Monica Vitti's wind swept hair on the island in *L'avventura*; Dorothy's electrified hair upon the arrival of the cyclone in *The Wizard of Oz*; Lillian Gish's hair blowing backwards in the 'Blue Norther' in *The Wind*; Marilyn Monroe's dress blowing up to her waistline on the subway in *The Seven Year Itch*; Maria Schneider's hair blowing in all directions on the roof of a moving Cadillac in *The Passenger* ... and the list goes on. Reflecting on this gesture and motif of my childhood, with its ensuing cinephiliac pleasures, brings me much embarrassment. I feel as if I am romanticising something much more serious. But it is not just the person themself that sparks my adoration, nor the fetishisation of wind-swept hair in particular, it is the dance between the human and nonhuman, and the need to join this continuum. The wind, through its distinct effect on the human in question, endows that person of whatever gender with an ultra-feminised, yet deeply impersonal vitality. As a child, I was fascinated by the TV series *Silas*. It chronicled the nomadic life of Silas, a child orphan and vagabond, who ran away on horseback from the circus. I vividly recall the feeling of ecstatic wonder that arose in me, when Silas, a beautiful, androgynous, long-haired boy, galloped furiously on his horse at the edge of the shoreline at dusk, fleeing the tyrant circus ringmaster, and the oppressive micro-regime of circus routine. The hair of horse and boy streamed wildly, as they rode together towards the unknown ... More recently, I had the opportunity to visit an exhibit at the British Museum in 2014 entitled, *Witches and Wicked Bodies*. To my surprise I discovered that a vast proportion of the women depicted in these medieval etchings, paintings, and sketches were of women with hair blowing in all directions, often accompanied by horses whose manes blew backward. However derogatory the intentions were behind these portrayals, it was striking to discover that there was an aesthetic heritage to my fascination. On one particular etching, entitled 'The Sorceress', by the seventeenth century German artist, Jan van de Velde; a woman is stooped over a cauldron preparing for the Sabbath in the company of other sentient beings and entities, including a goat, and a particularly grotesque looking demon. What animates the entire image is the woman's mane frozen mid-air, swept forward by a wicked wind; her hair taking flight beyond the confines of the pictorial frame.

Dalia Neis

1928 (The year of magical thinking) Manchester, The Penumbral Eclipse

A soft-neon light flooded though the dimly filtered windowpanes of the John Rylands library reading room; its green strobes cast a luminous shadow across the edge of my desk. I read this as an auspicious sign to take a break from the staid atmosphere of studious research. I was overcome by the familiar exhaustion of oppressive library stillness; the icy silence of the reading room was occasionally interrupted by curious tourists who took pictures on their mobile phones of the shrine-like, decaying splendour of the room, amidst researchers frozen in saintly gestures at their dust-infested alcoves, with their backs bent double over their yellowing manuscripts. Beckoned by the green light, I followed its translucent presence flashing in a hidden alley, leading me on a circuitous route to the entrance of a decaying workers' cafe with the neon green letters – NWSW – blinking above its crumbling doorway.

It was 18 October 2015, but it felt like 1928. I was transported by the lingering afterglow of Victor Sjöstrom's 1928 silent film *The Wind*, which I had seen the week before for the second time at the Northwest Picturehouse, and was in the midst of preparing to film a 'loose' adaptation of this wind-swept, Southwest frontier vision in the North of England. Across the Eden Valley, along the southern slope of Cross Fell, blows a ferocious wind named the 'Helm', forming a fierce parallel, albeit lesser known equivalent, to the 'Blue Norther' of the American Southwest. I had in mind to stay in the library till midnight, to immerse myself in Virginia Woolf's vision of totality in the North of England, transcribed in her 1928 essay, 'The Sun and the Fish'. I hoped to discover events that took place in the North of England in 1928, alongside the filming of *The Wind* in the American Southwest: parallel film, literary, or cosmic happenings that forged lateral connections beyond gaps in space.

The funding of my film had recently fallen through; the producers grew tired of what they termed as my 'never-ending research phase', and by the script's 'incommunicability on screen'. They wanted to know the precise genre of the unmade film, "It keeps changing form," whined the chief producer, "you conned us into thinking we were funding a period drama." Their frustrations were

Zephyrian Spools (An Essay, A Wind)

justified; I had initially proposed a 'shot by shot' re-make of *The Wind* in the Eden Valley, but became drawn to the silent film itself, which was filmed in the Mojave Desert on the Southwest frontier. I began to focus on Victor Sjöström's own trials and tribulations in readapting the original Dorothy Scarborough Great Plains novel into the heat and dust of the desert. The film crew had rented a wooden shack in Mojave, a sprawling settlement town located east of the Tehachapi Mountains, on the southwest edges of the desert. The core production team included performer and co-producer Lillian Gish; author and script consultant, Dorothy Scarborough; scriptwriter, Frances Marion; director, Victor Sjöström, and around forty additional 'extras' and technicians in total. By day, they left for the desert to shoot the film in the scorching heat, with temperatures rising to more than one hundred and fifteen degrees. There they busied themselves staging and summoning the Blue Norther of West Texas into the sparse valleys of the desert, with the technological aid of multiple wind generators and smoke machines.

I worked with washed-out, original production stills from the 1928 location of *The Wind*: photographic portraits of the film's star, Lillian Gish, standing delicately by a barbed-wired fence masked in a pair of goggles, her head wrapped tightly in a flowing scarf caught mid-flight; the film's director, Victor Sjöström; posing elegantly with the rest of the cast in front of giant wind-propellers; the entire film crew focusing intently on horses galloping into the desert horizon while wind machines beat sand into wild torrents.

Something 'happened' out there in the Mojave Desert with this film crew at this particular time and place. I was convinced that this film shoot was no ordinary Hollywood production; that it had flopped and damaged Lillian Gish's career in the process appealed to me even more. To my mind, this film crew were using film technology and wind propellers in much the same way that sorcerers used medicinal plants, or the way that time travellers escaped to other dimensions with machines built from scraps of metal. There was a sense that this film crew had collectively escaped the banalities of everyday existence, and had used the filmmaking process to jump into the unknown.

I tuned back into the seductive, faded aesthetics of the cafe's interior. There were cracked mirrors hanging from the walls, creating an effect of spatial elongation and distortion. Three lone traffic controllers sat in solitary red booths, their reflections multiplied as they sipped their tea in silence. Directly behind me, reflected in the cracks of the mirror, were two elderly women enjoying their afternoon tea:

"They never should have allowed you to go outside on the eve of the lunar eclipse, Beryl."

"But it's sunny and still today."

"We'll never forget the day you fell down the fell, tumbling down you were in that chill haunted weather back in the valley."

Tuning out of the two women's tea banter, I shifted away from the mirror maze, and focused my restless gaze on the view of the empty parking lot. 'The eve of the lunar eclipse … '. Soft strobes gently rippled the edges of the building's seams. The sky on this day took on a ceremonial quality, suffusing an ethereal texture to the gravity-bound frame of this city's brick and mortar. Even its inhabitants seemed more attuned to sky and weather. My attention to Northern weather re-triggered fragments from Virginia Woolf's essay, 'The Sun and the Fish'. The rhythm of her words faded in like luminous, sonic frequencies over the darkening shadows of the building's seams. I began to murmur out loud, in a semi-audible tone, the following passage:

> *All noses were pointing north. When for a moment we were halted in the depths of the country, there were the pale lights of motorcars also pointing north. All were traveling north. All were thinking of the dawn.*

Beams of electric lights flickered sporadically in between the building's seams. I then recited fragments from the transitional passage out loud, hoping that no one in the café would notice my sudden prayer-like eruption:

> *We were no longer in the same relation to people, houses, and trees; we were related to the whole world. We were come not to lodge ourselves in the bedroom of an inn; we were come for a few hours of disembodied intercourse with the sky.*

The sky permeates Woolf's writing. She points to the sky as a channel for receiving and gleaning knowledge – a knowledge that cannot be found in the designated institutions of the library, the academy, or the domestic sphere. Woolf (along with her collective eclipse gathering), had come to escape from the hierarchical limitations of the human world, by entering into an immanent world of abstraction, sensual awareness, and collective solidarity with the sky itself … the total eclipse of the sun elicits a form of sexuality that is simultaneously depersonalised, planetary, and orgiastic. Out of domesticity, into totality's abyss.

Zephyrian Spools (An Essay, A Wind)

In *A Room of One's Own*, Woolf's narrator/alter-ego's epiphanies break out precisely when outside in the streets, or while looking through the window 'at the stream of things'. Woolf's own meandering preparation for her Newnham Women's College lecture series, reached its peak, when, on one 'unproductive afternoon' in 1928, she left the British Library rather suddenly, and sought momentary refuge in a dimly lit cafe where she sat looking through its panoramic windows at the sky. It was at that moment when everything clicked into place for her. It happened through the detours, during those marginal moments – from library reading room, to caffeine-induced sky watching.

Something 'happened' to Woolf on that Yorkshire hillside where she crossed a threshold of the senses, paralleling the initiation rites of Antonin Artaud's hallucinogenically inspired Mexico experiences in 1935, where the 'Rite of the Black Sun' passages echo Woolf's own writings on the solar eclipse. Whereas Artaud is preoccupied with immortalising totality's blackout, Woolf's writing on the eclipse celebrates the transitional passageway from planetary blackout to its recuperation of colour and light, 'How then does light return to the world after the eclipse of the sun?'

Just before heading back to the library, I took a final walk during the last moments of light. I walked straight through the alleyway leading back to the library and slowly re-traced my steps down Deansgate, in the direction of Castlefield and the forking paths of the Rochdale and Bridgewater Canals. On the river banks; Deansgate-Castlefield spread out before me, an enigmatic labyrinth of time pockets, encompassing folds of ruins and hidden shrines to forgotten goddesses and persecuted warriors, whose ashen remains lay scattered alongside newly developed housing complexes. Back westward in Toad Street – formerly known as Toad Lane – lay the debris of the home of the Shaker pioneer Ann Lee. Only a vestige of her crumbling dwelling remained buried under the railway tracks of the newly renovated Victoria Station. The city's multiple layers in time and space unraveled before me, a lucid maze, its shadowy past now rendered visible by the distinct atmosphere of a place and time. The colour of translucent red Ivy submerged on a former decaying cotton mill on the other side of the docks. To my left, within the nexus of the Mamucium, lay the patch of Roman ruins, its fort and earlier remnants of the pagan temple of Mithras fell down the wayside below the newly constructed office blocks, exposing the neon sign of Starbucks with the vivacious glow of the iconic mermaid. I began to crave caffeine, perhaps semi-seduced by the G-rated icon of the siren, but resisted the temptation to cross the bridge for a quick fix. To my right, below the docks, a boat of solemn tourists sailed past, an enclosed gaudy leopard-patterned barge floated calmly ahead, and from my peripheral vision I caught a glimpse of a pink translucent globe. The moon's presence chimed a ritual threshold crossing of day to night. It was the beginning of the lunar eclipse. The Northern sky on this late afternoon was a lunar counterpart to Woolf's solar eclipse sky of 1928. Rather than ordinary clock time, it was as if the North of England in 1928, and the North of England in 2015, merged at this moment into a fluid sky entity, becoming solar-lunar shades of one boundless continuum, with its shifting rhythm of wind, clouds, suns, moons, and stars. I walked past a series of abandoned warehouses and cotton mills with luminous graffiti and rich murals sprawled over concrete remains of factory walls. '*Save us from gravity*', read one graffiti refrain, '*Disappear into the cracks*', read another. I climbed up the steps leaving the Bridgewater Canal behind me, leading me across the Thelwall Viaduct, directly to the dreary M6 motorway, towards the Ship Canal, where the Irwell River flows into the Irish Sea. The sky above me grew more charged with its sweeping clouds, its drooping pink canopy veined with threads of light reflected by the waning sun and the rapidly rising moon. The streets were empty, and I walked across narrow footbridges and empty parking lots, always following the direction of the moon, continually perplexed by its over-bearing presence and odd luminosity.

'Silent Cinema's Sublime Winds'

– Voice-over of Dr. Lizzie Zephyrah over molecular pixels and digital storms

In order to comprehend the constellation of the elements – the voices of wind in the medium of film – let us hearken back to the primordial world of its ghostly beginnings, when the mists of formless air stalked the cinema screens, in which primordial space contracted infinite light, to allow the virtual-real space of cinematic flight.

In the beginning of the beginning there was the air and atmosphere – a formless void of stirring gases, molecular and plasmatic – a gaping hole from which seeped the fantastic.

The space of 'empty matter' is never dead, but charged with a breath of another kind, conjoined gusts of pixelated air, streaming upwards and out, de-accelerated sound, followed by a heliospheric pause, before slipping into layers of glitched-out spores.

The void shimmers with solar winds – its sub-atomic particles pulsate planets, galaxies and alien stars. Waves of air become lake-borne energy. Human and non-human particles intertwine, forging a glacial matrix of the virtual-divine. Gases of *machinic* winds pulsate pre-historic rocks with a dense, brewing fog, which the late, great, film critic, Lotte Eisner, named *Sfumato*.

The wind is created from an alchemy of weather. Out of doors and out of breath we glean the night sky. The wind is an empty frame from which activity of this force becomes a name. The kabbalists remind us that creation is made up of words and the forces of nature. *Ruh*, breath, *Ruach*, spirit, *Nefesh*, air, *Neshama*, wind, *Tzimzum*, limitless light, the wind's refracted sight.

Dalia Neis

The Empty Frame

I found Dr. Lizzie Zephyrah on one of my marathon Google searches. I entered the following key words: 'women scholars, silent cinema', then 'silent cinema & the weather', then 'women scholars, silent cinema, & the weather', followed by 'wind & film'. I had 7 hits. The first two hits were a couple of noted scholarly books, Kristi Mckim's *Cinema as Weather*, and Davinia Quinlivan's *The Place of Breath in Cinema*. Then I found Dr. Lizzie Zephyrah, and a link to her book of film criticism, entitled, *Silent Cinema's Sublime Winds*. That was it. I hit the jackpot roulette of internet searches. I freeze framed the title and took a screen shot, several screen shots, and then proceeded to google once more, this time with a clear focus in mind: "Dr. Lizzie Zephyrah, Silent Cinema's Sublime Winds." It was like an anagram had unfolded. There were lots of silent cinema hits, 2 hits on sublime winds, but nothing related to Dr. Lizzie Zephyrah. I googled Dr. Lizzie Zephyrah once more. This time I had a hit. It was a profile of her with a little more detail, which exposed a blurry portrait of a woman with ruffled, unruly hair, with an elegant white streak at the center. Dr. Lizzie Zephyrah was based in the north of England, in the region of the Eden Valley; she was vaguely 'affiliated' with the University of Cumbria, although she had no apparent, official, lecturing post there – 'Oh wow, Susan Sontag of the North!' In the photo, her gaze had a strange austerity to it, as if she was looking at something far off frame. I zoomed in closer, as close as I could, the image became pixelated, then zap, the computer screen blanked out. It had a meltdown. I tried to turn it on, but it didn't blink. Dr Lizzie Zephyrah refused to be stalked any further. I waited, smoked a cigarette, and took the opportunity to absorb my recent virtual discovery. It was almost as good as discovering the Helm wind, almost as revelatory as discovering the Sjöstrom film. It felt like I might have found my weather-born, cinematic soul-mate.

'Silent Cinema's Sublime Winds – The Unfilmable' (excerpt #3)

> We are mad to be filming the wind. It's like filming the impossible. We are mad to be filming the wind; filming the impossible is what's best in life. All of my life I have tried. I have tried to capture, to tame the wind.
>
> – Joris Ivens, *Une Historie De Vent* (1988)

Uttering this refrain from out of his asthmatic ninety-year old frame, the Dutch filmmaker, Joris Ivens, looks back at his prolific career, sweeping from the peaks of silent cinema, all the way up to the end of the 20th century. Ivens explores his longstanding fascination with wind through the apophatic lens of the negative theologian. Negative theology's logic of deflection, denial, and detours, acknowledges the impossibility of knowing God or describing the numinous experience. We are mad to film the wind, so let us film the rain.

In Joris Ivens' silent film, *Regen* (1929), Amsterdam is drenched with torrential outpours. The rain is depicted in abstract geometrical forms, here as a reflection on a pane of glass, and there as an outpouring of transparent blades over a plane of mass-moving, rotating umbrellas. We are mad to film the wind, so let us film the rain. In Joris Ivens' silent film, *Regen* (1929), Amsterdam is drenched with torrential outpours. The rain is depicted in abstract geometrical forms, here as a reflection on a pane of glass, and there as an outpouring of transparent blades over a plane of mass-moving, rotating umbrellas.

The wind flutters suddenly before the storm erupts; a restless breeze rattles the window frames, and the shirts, skirts, and pantalones blow up with life on the clothing line. An abstraction of rain unfolds through curious perspectives, and shadowy reflected forms. The wind becomes a film-extra on-screen, animating the flat surfaces, with a charged and unexpected form of vitality.

The filmmaker's final documentary, *Une Histoire de Vent* (1988) – as the title suggests, a deliberate, direct, cinematic meditation on wind – falls flat in comparison to *Regen's* peculiar, evocative charge. In the latter film, Ivens attempts to capture the wind on frame: re-staging his journey to China where he consults Daoist sages about the relationship between breath, air, and breeze, creating laborious, fantastical wind reenactments which unfold in between the sand dunes of the Gobi desert; but *Une Histoire de Vent* ends on a stagnant, windless note. The struggles of filming the wind are apparent, but very little of the wind itself comes through. Instead the wind is collapsed into a purely mythical, symbolic plane; its animated breath is flattened in the contours of a cinematic frame. A doomed negative theologian, Ivens performs a task unmet; a life-long, failed quest to film the wind.

There exists a long-standing tradition of mystics, writers, and artists who were or are captivated by ways in which to represent the ineffable; their failed attempts shape the very urgency of their inquiry, often, in the process, crossing thresholds of expressive modes and aesthetic forms. The medieval Benedictine nun, Hildegard von Bingen, forms part of this legacy, with her apophatic visions of the divine.[*] In her multi-disciplinary works the proto-media-artist nun turns to musical composition, poetry, pharmaceutical treatise, and revelationary accounts, as a means to strike open a passage to the divine. She does this via a performance of negation, doubt, and self-deprecating humility. In order to speak about her relationship to God she draws from the language of the natural elements. In order to describe the divine she turns to the wind. In order to contemplate the healing attributes of wind she speaks about its cosmic force and Godly powers. In her painting entitled 'The Cosmic Tree' (1152)[†] Hildegard von Bingen paints an intricate, multilayered, circular tableaux, in which she herself is present in the corner of the circular frame, breathing out a divine force, which is the painting itself with its spherical visions. It's almost as if the world of the physical painting, and the world of the metaphysical, collapses into an amorphous, temporal glitch, much like the miraculous momentum of a future cinema yet to exist.

Everything burns because of me in such a way as our breath constantly moves us, like the wind-tossed flame in a fire."[‡] Von Bingen, in this pantheistic refrain, straddles imperceptibly from a first-person "I" to a collective "we", while posing the question: what cosmic powers are imparted through the winds of the cardinal

---

[*] Hildegard von Bingen (1098-1179), also known as Saint Hildegard of the Rhine, was a German mystic and polymath. Some historians say that von Bingen painted the illustrations, others argue that she dictated her visions in a trance, while the nuns transcribed them into diagrams and paintings.

[†] Another of von Bingen's trance-induced illuminations, featured in the lost manuscript, *Scivias* (1175).

[‡] Anne Lenzmeier-King,*Hildegard of Bingen: An Integrated Vision* (Michael Glazier Press, Wilmington, 2001), p.65.

points? We cannot know, but we are now in a space in much closer proximity to the wind's elusive presence.

The filmmaker Joris Ivens stands on the other side of this spectrum with a whip on his back. In an analogous vein, the filmmaker doubts his own ability to capture the invisible image of wind. However, unlike Hildegard von Bingen's sublimated visions, Ivens is neither schooled nor refined in the aesthetic and visionary modes of divine translation. Rather than embodying the language of denial, and transposing the medium of film into a sublime game of anti-representation (as von Bingen would no doubt do), Ivens merely reaches the first level of apophatic prayer. He, unlike the Benedictine nun, remains in the purgatory state of literal exposure: it does not suffice to deny one's effort to represent the wind – one needs to tune into the invisible plain, where the senses coordinate a dance beyond the ocular frame.

Dalia Neis

The Magic Stone

When I first laid eyes on Dr. Lizzie Zephyrah, as she sat poised over the damp earth, planting herbs and seeds in an open field leading up to her home at the foot of the Eden Valley, I was certain that I recognised her from a screening of *The Wind* at the Northwest Picturehouse. On this distinctly windless afternoon, Dr. Zephyrah motioned to me to sit on the ground beside her. Without a word between us we sat crouched in between the crooked boulders. We played silently with the soft soil, fumbling with the roots and seeds on a patch of damp earth, planting sage, plantain, mint, catnip, mugwort, nettle and thyme seeds, surrounded by an abundance of lady's mantle, bird's eye primrose, teesdale violets, and shady horsetails. I noticed how diligently Dr. Zephyrah handled the soil, seeds and plants; she was both meticulous yet thoroughly intimate, as if she were grooming and nurturing an extension of her own body.

"On the first afternoon of my arrival at the farm," I began to tell Dr. Zephyrah about my stay at Dufton Farm with my host, Trudy Foster, as she continued the rest of the seeding process alone, "Trudy sat at the end of my bed and proceeded to narrate a long, delirious, monologue on her various encounters with the Helm wind over the last thirty years of living in the Eden Valley. She seemed to take great pleasure in telling me about the arrogance of the various lone-male guests who took it upon themselves – against her advice – to venture out to the top of Cross Fell in fierce, windy weather. Each of these men had met their fates on their respective escapades, mostly in fatal injury – "One of whom," she remarked in a deadpan tone, "was simply blown off the top of the fell, and found later the same afternoon, sprawled on Mr Kleidly's farm, with boots, hats, and coat intact." I noticed later that evening on the way back to my room in the farm, refreshed after a long walk up to High Cup Nick, that the sprawling, never-ending corridor walls of the farmhouse were eerily lined with newspaper clippings of various men who were crushed by the Helm. On another newspaper cutting, one walker – another guest of Trudy's farmhouse – decided to venture to High Cup Nick on the afternoon of the autumn equinox, and was promptly blown off the ridge when the biting Helm erupted. Pasted haphazardly on top of this cutting, was a washed out, crudely-cut page from the local Cumbrian paper, which featured an account of three men who had fallen off Cross Fell – one spring day in 1928, the Helm had tossed them to the valley below."

Dr. Zephyrah continued to plant the seeds carefully while listening attentively to my account. After a long silence, she finally spoke: "On the one hand it is important to uncover the arrogance of these men in the face of their obliviousness to wind, but on the other … "

Dr. Zephyrah paused mid-sentence, swiveling her hips to face the opposite direction, with views to the open valley. I slowly turned to face the direction of her gaze – northeast, over the valley range, beyond the glades, towards the Cross Fell escarpment in the distance; its peak vanishing into a vortex of mist and steam.

"Cross Fell was formerly known as Fiend's Fell," Dr. Zephyrah continued at last, "the inhabitants of the Northern Pennines attributed the voice of the Helm to the breath of the devil, and considered the fell to be a cursed entity. This fell was later exorcised by a priest, who renamed it 'Cross Fell'. Just as we have denuded this terrain of its trees, we have denuded this wind's vastness, designating it to a categorical corner of our mind, projecting it as a transcendental malignant force, an entity outside, and separate from us. We need to embody a Spinozist approach to wind … " Dr. Zephyrah remarked in an enigmatic, scholarly tone, and slowly turned back around to sit facing me. "There are other faces to this wind. The wind is composed of particles of matter. Yet it is also sublime – how do you demystify, reveal and not show at the same time?"

Before I had a chance to respond to what seemed like a rhetorical question Dr. Zephyrah began to carve off a small shard of sandstone with a penknife revealing to me a labyrinth of extraordinary patterns at the stone's core. There were swirling, spherical lines crossing its heart. I examined the intricate nature of its vortex design as she continued to speak. "What makes the Victor Sjöstrom film so unique is that even – and in spite of its depiction of the brutal force of wind in the barren lands of the Great Plains, and the female protagonist's apparent ensuing mental disintegration – beyond this wind's particular destructive qualities, its avenging force, its transcendental qualities, lies another direction to its power."

I continued to be absorbed in the swirling, wave-shaped patterns of the rock; they began to take on a diagrammatic significance, forming a spiralling equivalent to her words.

"We see the Blue Norther slowly enfolding Lillian Gish's body … and we see that through this sudden unexpected caress, that the wind, too, becomes transformed … "

At this last sentence, Dr. Zephyrah's voice trailed off. As if to demonstrate what she had just explained to me, her silk scarf fell effortlessly to the floor, while her thick, wavy hair tousled down the nape of her neck, and began to rustle softly in a breeze that had sprung from nowhere. I sat crouched down next to her, moving in closer. I shifted my gaze from the animated swirls of the wind blasted rock to her hands attending to the earth as she planted the remaining seeds. Her hair was now blowing in all directions, her eyes blazed with intense concentration on the task at hand. Then the entire field took on a sudden burst of life and began to sway in rhythmic acknowledgment to her words. She looked to me at this moment, I thought, like a witch or resistance fighter from another era, one that had survived the many phases of persecution in this land. Dr. Zephyrah began to whistle an eerie melody; it sounded as if it was transmitted from a remote past, where melodies have the amorphous texture of oneiric incantation and sensual revelation; she then proceeded to sing an Orphic hymn, dedicated to the Northern winds:

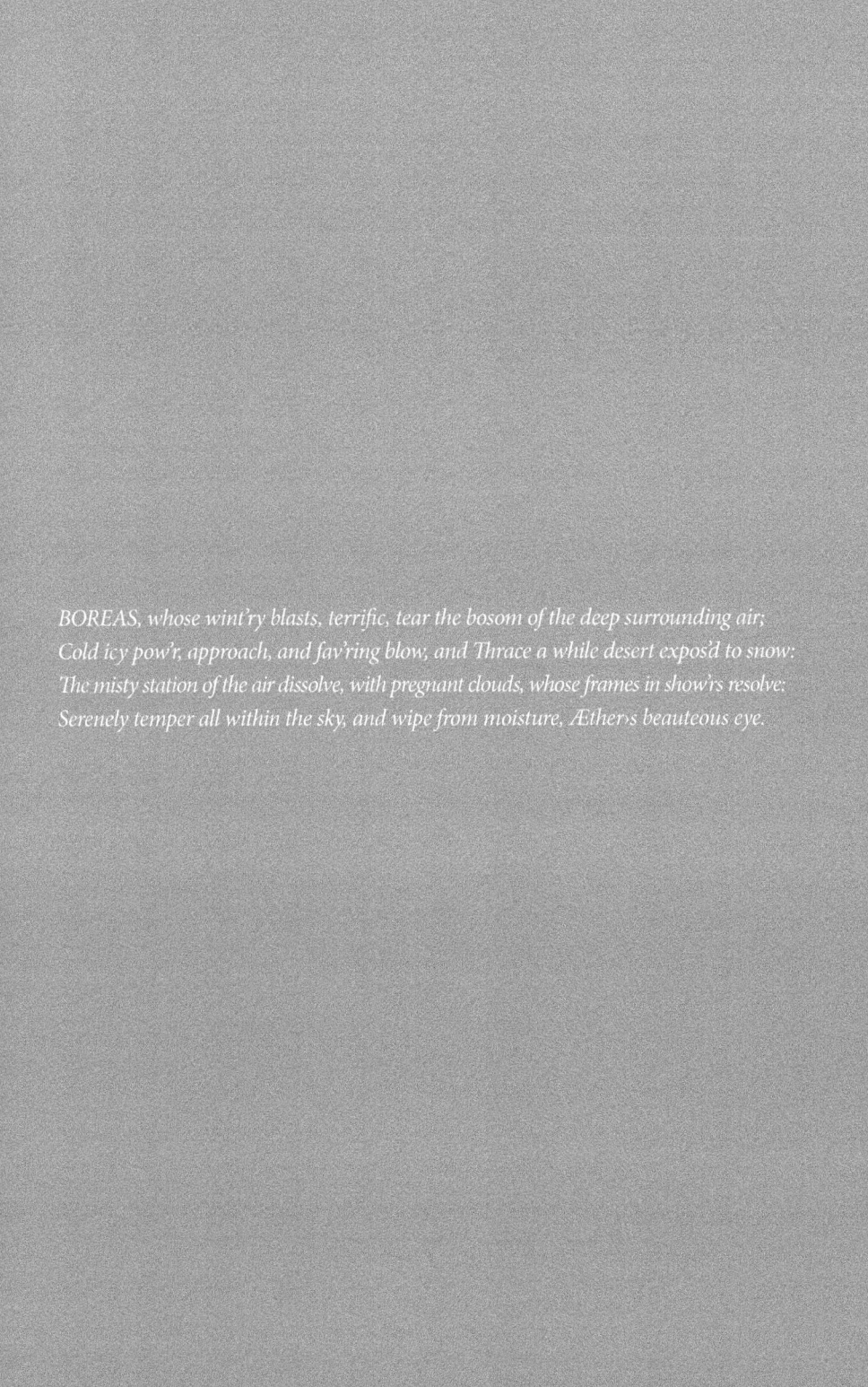

BOREAS, whose wint'ry blasts, terrific, tear the bosom of the deep surrounding air;
Cold icy pow'r, approach, and fav'ring blow, and Thrace a while desert expos'd to snow:
The misty station of the air dissolve, with pregnant clouds, whose frames in show'rs resolve:
Serenely temper all within the sky, and wipe from moisture, Æther›s beauteous eye.

Zephyrian Spools (An Essay, A Wind)

'Silent Cinema's Sublime Winds – Spinozist Visions' (excerpt #4)

In *Pour le Mistral* (1966), Joris Ivens deploys multiple cinematic techniques to evoke, invoke, explain, expose, and frame the wind. Among these techniques are high-angled point of view shots filmed from helicopters in the sky: the camera zaps through the clouds, gazing down on earth and its inhabitants below; static shots of debris caused by the Mistral's destruction; swaying camera shots of tree-trunks sliced by wind; freeze frames of villagers caught in trembling anticipation; a young girl's neck tenses as she stands, isolated in an arid meadow. The camera's point of view combines with a God like voice-over: "One day I will offer you mastery of the weather," the narrator booms in a biblical tone, over images of remote landscapes, amidst the trepidation of the impending storm.

The name 'Mistral' is derived from the Latin *Magistralis*: meaning 'masterly', a fitting name for this particular wind's temperament, which howls like a jet stream, sometimes at 150 kilometres an hour, down through the valley of the Rhone. Ivens' film works with an equivalent cinematic technique, which attempts, in turn, to *master* the *Mistral*, and the gaze of the spectator, "It will rain, shine and storm like a ballet. It will rage cyclones in a pretty row. It will make green shepherd's pipes spring from this sunny Saharan tomb. One day I will offer you mastery of the weather," booms the gruff voice. *Pour le Mistral* masters our eyes and ears through a controlling cinematic gaze, leaving us in an overwhelmed, and ultimately washed out haze.

In the films of Jean Marie Straub and Danièlle Huillet, the opposite takes place: rather than framing the wind, these filmmakers move the frame. If Ivens is a self-conscious, negative theologian, with a transcendentalist bent, then the Straub/Huillet duo are neo-Spinozists of the materialist frame. If we are to consider the duo, Spinozist-materialist filmmakers, it is because, they – like the seventeenth century philosopher and lens grinder, Baruch Spinoza – render the imperceptible visible.* They, like their lens-grinder

---

* Baruch Benedictus Spinoza (1632-1677) was a Dutch optical pioneer and philosopher Spinoza's approach to lens-grinding provoked rich metaphysical questions on visuality, and bore a striking contrast to the popular Cartesian lens-grinding techniques of the time. Spinoza insisted on grinding panoramic lenses instead of the common hyperbolic lenses pioneered by René Descartes.

predecessor, express an optical curiosity for neglected, imperceptible forces that lie on the periphery, and opt for a wide-panoramic vision, with very little concern for what lies in the centre of the frame. This is a striking antithesis to a Cartesian, optical approach, in which the central axis of vision is foregrounded with sharp-focused clarity, at the expense of the margins and the wider perspective of the whole.

Unlike Ivens' controlling camera gaze – or his later attempts to frame the wind as an illusory force, invoking the pioneering trickery and magic of George Méliès – the Straub/Huillet films hark back to the counter-pioneering minimal efforts of Augustus and Louis Lumière. Their films are twitching, vibrating canvases of the world arriving, as if, for the first time. In Straub/Huillet's Spinozist-cinematic output there is no omnipotent god, and there is no transcendental wind; they refuse to fixate on the wind as a central subject, and do not seek to frame the wind at the expense of other living matter and natural forces in the frame. Referring to Ivens in an interview, Huillet remarks, "The wind, Ivens took it as his theme, and that's a recipe for disaster. What happens then always happens by some kind of contraband. You never thought 'I want to film the wind.'"[†] Yet despite Huillet's explicit objection to Ivens' attempt to frame the wind, Straub/Huillet's own films – in particular, *Too Early, Too Late* (1982) – are subtle cinematic odes to wind; they are deeply engaged with the imperceptible forces and atmospheres of the material world. This holds true whether in the soft murmur of a stream and the passing of a cloud in *Antigone* (1992), or the sound of insects, and the wind rustling the trees in *Too Early, Too Late*, their films function as moving testimonies to the natural world, where human and nonhuman co-inhabit the frame. When interviewers ask the filmmaker duo about their approach to the material world they often resort to quoting the silent film director D.W. Griffith, "What the modern movie lacks is beauty – the beauty of moving wind in the trees."[‡] For Straub/Huillet, the landscape, the wind, the clouds, and the atmosphere form a palimpsest of a terrain's history; its ruined eroded presence is how we bear witness to its name. The film's utmost material detail de-tunes our senses, and flips them out, re-tuning us to other dimensions previously too minute and imperceptible to follow. The French film critic, Serge Daney refers to these cinematic magnifications as the "audio hallucinatory" texture of their

---

[†] Hans Hurch, "Too Early, Too Late: Interview with Huillet and Straub" (1984), trans. Ben Brewster

[‡] *Ibid.*

films, in which he draws an earlier comparison to silent cinema's sublime winds, in particular, to Victor Sjöström's mute "stormscapes" in *The Wind* (1928).[§]

For Straub/Huillet, the wind may seem strictly peripheral, yet it makes its presence known in *Too Early, Too Late*, as a binding thread across time and space. The landscape of breathing wind is a palimpsest of the histories of revolution in France on the one hand – characterised through slow panning shots of blades of grass blowing gently across a meadow, and in Egypt, on the other – captured in dust blown shots by the River Nile. Both these sequences simultaneously refer to the imperceptible minor winds of the material world, as well as to the sweeping whirlwinds of historical revolutions.

Walter Benjamin's visions of wind in Marseille, in the summer of 1928, while sitting at a café at night by the old port, were at their most euphoric when he was high *on hashish*.[**] His trances arose when he experienced not the drama of the Mistral, but when he sat bewitched by the gentle zephyr blowing into a lace canopy, "For the trance always begins with laughter, or some times with a less noisy, more inward, but more joyous laughter. And now I recognised it by the infinite tenderness of the wind that was blowing the fringes of the curtain on the opposite side of the street."[††] Benjamin employs the German word *Rausch* translated into English as 'trance'. The German verb *Rauchen* carries additional onomatopoeic associations with the wind: it also means 'to rustle, roar, rush, murmur, thunder' as much as it means 'to trance out'. This joyous proclamation forms an affirmative counterpart to his later apocalyptic declaration in his 'Theses on the Philosophy of History' (1940), where, "[...] a storm is blowing from Paradise; it has got caught in his wings with such violence that the angel can no longer close them." Rather than the gentle zephyr, or the whirlwinds of historical revolution, here we have an ominous chronicle of the storm of progress. Paul Klee's painting, *Angelus Novus* (1920), to which this statement refers, depicts an angel frozen in a limbo glance, its gaze fixed outwards beyond the pictorial frame, its wings are blown backwards, as the debris of history grows into an uncontrollable storm of progress and impending

---

[§] For his conception of "audio hallucinations" in the cinema, in particular relation to Sjöström's The Wind, and Straub/Huillet's Too Early Too Late, see Serge Daney's essay "Cinemeteorology: Too Early Too Late" trans. Jonathan Rosenbaum (1982).

[**] Walter Benjamin experimented extensively with hashish, and was convinced that his most lucid philosophical and literary insights arose out of these trance experiences, which he termed "profane illuminations".

[††] Walter Benjamin, "Myslovice-Braunschweig-Marseille" (1928), in Howard Eiland (ed. and trans.), *On Hashish* (Cambridge, MA: Harvard University Press, 2006), p.111.

doom. The laughter of the hashish trance fades away[‡‡] as imperceptibly as its gentle arrival, blown over by greater and fiercer storms.

We tend to home in on destruction – as with Ivens' film, Pour le Mistral, as with Hollywood disaster films such as *Twister*, or the more recent blockbuster flop, *Into the Storm*. But rarely do we cast our cinematic gaze on to the varied voices of wind. The palette of wind frequencies is largely overlooked: those gentle zephyric breezes, those warm chinooks and sea breezes. In Sjöstrom's *The Wind*, it is not merely the destructive twister that is framed (which is anyway depicted in dark-shadowy forms, reflecting our imaginary projections, before bouncing back into our own echo chamber of sounds), it is equally the curious dancing reflection of storm in Lillian Gish's eyes, and the strand of her hair that falls suddenly, as she stands gazing out of the window contemplating her eventual surrender to the eye of the cyclone. Straub/Huillet, and Sjöstrom in turn, form part of a constellation of artists and writers who pay attention to the movement of air in all its multifaceted dimensions, to the sounds we don't ordinarily hear, and to the wind's effect on the minuscule features of the landscape. They form part of an ongoing tradition that harks back to the silent cinema, and to that era's preoccupation with elemental landscapes. Spinoza would certainly approve of their working methods, ordaining their cinematic oeuvre as a celebratory expression of the 'white fire of substance' – the eternal, axiomatic, cosmic wind.

[‡‡] Hölderlin's translation of Sophocles: "In them the harmony of the languages is so profound that sense is touched by language only the way an Aeolian harp is touched by the wind" Walter Benjamin's "The Task of the Translator" in *Illuminations*, trans. Harry Zohn (London: Fontana Press, 1969), p.82. Hölderlin himself declared that he was transformed for the better after being struck by a lightening storm on top of a mountain in France. Everything afterwards had altered: a new poetics emerged, elemental and stratospheric.

Post   Vision©

The frame becomes a canvas from which the world arrives.
Lay the camera on a tripod and turn on the power.
Cover the lens with a burning canopy.

From a sudden, amorphous plain the camera stumbles and falls –
slipping through the bubbling bog, acupuncturists tune into faded nerves
and tension points, swarming perfunctory cells ooze out pixilated spores
through sacred layers of folded skin.

Reels of skin unfold into the eye of a temporal storm, rewinding back
into the moving matrix of frozen futures, glitched-out memories
speak in alien tongues – vivid oranges, neon blues – outside the mark
of your language.

Reformulated joy unpacked into strips of pixilated psalms.
Burning canopy of suns, wolves recapitulating your human remains.

Dalia Neis

There was once a young girl
who flowed with the luminous crescent
of a full-bodied moon

She swayed with the flowing stream
into an eye of the crimson forest

                          The spirit of extinct animals
                          the pouakai, chamitataxus
                          forests of birch and pine
                          began to appear to her
                          as transparent film

Under the canopy of bare stars
she moved to the rhythm of the cardinal directions
under the cryptic instructions of the wind
she walked East-South
then South-West
followed by North-West

                    She lay down and felt the soft moss on her bare skin
                    her body feeling more pleasure
                    than any of her suitors' caresses

                                      Polydirectional
                                          joy
                                      came upon her

Zephyrian Spools (An Essay, A Wind)

A warm purple light
shot through her
swirling around her thighs

The moon was full and shone brightly on her face
everything was luminous
she saw dancing swallows gliding in the sky
somersaulting and free falling
gliding vertically with tremendous speed
only to reach greater heights into the stratosphere

A golden pheasant landed on her belly
the wind, plants and birds
began to call out her names
"Lydia, Lillian, Lizzie, Lilith"

In the nocturnal depths of the moonless spheres
shining above the deep shifting clouds
white stallions gallop across the galaxy-strewn night
whatever happened to the original wind dancers?

In whose golden land did the grass grow and the cattle graze?
what happened to the original feather-like memory of Lilit
whose name invokes the Mesopotamian storm spirit
of Ancient Sumer, circa 3000 bce
Lilit, Lilake, Lilitu, Lilim, Lilot, Lilith, Lilis, Lil.

Dalia Neis

Memories of a Northern Wind

I studied filmmaking in FAMU – the Czech National Photography, Film, and Television Academy in Prague. My migration from northwest London to Prague seemed like a 'logical' step for my interests and creative pursuits; studying the craft of cinema in this context excited my cinephilic obsession with films made in that part of Europe. I loved, in varying degrees of intensity – Věra Chytilová, Jan Švankmajer, Jan Němec, and Miloš Forman – who were all former graduates and sporadic faculty members of FAMU. There were also the regular workshops, symposiums, and public lectures delivered by guest international scholars and filmmakers, including regular visits by the American filmmaker and essayist, Susan Sontag, who held the academy and its aesthetic legacy in high esteem. I remember a particular talk that she gave in a dingy classroom at the back of the photography department to a modest crowd of curious students. This talk, which was more of a smoke-ridden, informal conversation than a straightforward, conventional lecture, began with Sontag probing the young students in the room about their thoughts on contemporary media representations of women in the Czech Republic. Most of the students looked blank and gave vague and embarrassed responses to her question. When the turn came for me to speak I looked at her and realised that this might be the first time that someone had asked me a question like this.

I came out stuttering an incomprehensible series of fever-induced sentences, which then morphed into an inspired rant, followed by an indignant sermon. After the talk I approached her at the basement café of the school, and we had a brief but intense exchange about our mutual interests in cinema, and my filmmaking ambitions in particular. As she left, she looked at me silently, holding a piercing gaze before stating that 'I must continue to pursue this cinema obsession at all costs', and swiftly left the room, leaving me pining for her ever since.

That year in Prague formed a key rite of passage into questionings of my sexuality, as well as an awakening of what I understand now to be a coming into being of my feminist consciousness. I had narrowly escaped a marriage ceremony in which I was to be the potential bride of an 'eligible' Jewish doctor, and had decided to rupture this thread, and let myself go in another direction by throwing myself into a central European capital city filled with ghosts of my ancestors. That year in Prague was filled with intellectual epiphanies and creative quests. It was the year when I forged a filmmaking aesthetic that arose out of a rich discourse in cinema history, coupled with a personal and metaphysical investigation into my cultural origins.

At the end of my year in Prague I departed by train to the neighbouring border of Poland to make a film about my missing uncle, Meilich Last. Meilich was the only member of his generation who remained in Poland since the second-world-war; all traces of him had vanished and his whereabouts had never since been discovered. I was intrigued by the taboo and secrecy that surrounded him, and the enigmatic silence whenever I uttered his name to my older relatives, triggering a series of unanswered questions and psychic apparitions.

At FAMU I met and studied with the visiting lecturer of aesthetics, Rabbi Sascha Vodič, an avid cinephile and theorist. He was the Rabbi of the local Jewish community in Kraków, and commuted on a weekly basis to Prague. We connected over our mutual love for experimental film and independent cinema histories. I would enjoy challenging Rabbi Vodič about the role of images and visuality in Judaism, and how this contradicted or supported his love for the cinema.

"But as an Orthodox Jew, Rabbi Vodič, how do you marry your love for movies with the traditional prohibition of image representation?"

"Lydia, there is nothing *halachically* wrong with watching films if it brings you closer to God. I think you'll need to explore more thoroughly the history of visuality in Judaism. We have plenty of images, just not direct, literal representations of God. We 'see' things through parables and myths. Think of the best experimental filmmakers – their use of montage, *mise-en-scene*, and narration combine to resonate with the most profound midrashic tales!"

We would have different variations of these dialogues on a weekly basis at the basement canteen of FAMU. I began to slowly introduce Rabbi Vodič to my own filmmaking aspirations, and spoke to him about my plans for shooting a film in Poland. Weeks later, I was housesitting for Rabi Vodič at his Krakow home. I watered his plants and fed his children's pet rabbits, while he and his family hosted an intensive community workshop in Warsaw for the summer.

During this period I feverishly wrote my 'film script,' which was inspired by a DVD binge of Tarkovsky films that were left in a pile by Rabbi's Vodič's

TV set. I became fascinated by the filmmaker's recurring use of elemental motifs: the sound of water and wind, the microscopic attention to the earth, and the floating camera sequences in the sky. I watched all of his film works over one weekend, and began promptly to rearrange my script, incorporating elemental techniques borrowed from Tarkovsky's oeuvre, while drawing from the 'psychodramatic' tropes from my recent discovery in Prague of Maya Deren's experimental films. Unlike Tarkovsky's macho mysticism, I was drawn to Deren on a much deeper, libidinal level. And although I never actually understood her films (which seemed to be cryptic and obscure gestures of cinematic divination), Deren became some kind of mentor to me; she seemed to hold the key to a charged, feminine aesthetic, an aesthetic that was alien yet compelling. I later grew out of her stubborn polemical stance and her films' unwavering opacity, yet Deren formed a key part of my feminist awakening, and reminded me of the significance of aligning myself to women and the legacies of marginalised, ecstatic voices. The entire filmmaking process that summer became a delirious interior exploration of my ancestral origins, while I grappled for the appropriate cinematic tools to invoke, conjure up, and awaken this history through myself as filmmaker/protagonist/medium.

I remember sitting with Rabbi Vodič at his weekly Friday night dinners at the synagogue, after his return from Warsaw. We were having a heated debate about Tarkovsky.

"How do you marry Tarkovsky's mystical Christian beliefs with your own Jewish beliefs?"

"Tarkovsky was more of a pagan, and I myself am more of a Chassidic pantheist. We are not poles apart, Lydia. I feel closer to him than many of my Rabbinic peers."

Rabbi Vodič's response to my question reassured me, and although I was in the midst of leaving all remnants of my religious, orthodox, Jewish background behind me, I shared his pantheist, cinephilic visions, and considered him to be my third ally, along with Andrei Tarkovsky and Maya Deren, by generously opening his home to me so that I might explore my creative process, and concentrate fully on my filmmaking project.

My film *Missing Meilich* was shot on out-of-date, black and white 8mm film stock, on a second-hand, wind-up camera. For most of this film I was incognito, dressed in black, and got my cinematographer (fellow film student), to film me as I walked through archives and derelict bridges, bathed in the bathtub, lay on a bed in dingy hotel rooms, sat in a café contemplating, danced in circles in the town square embracing a Torah scroll, and pouted in a medieval Jewish cemetery by a gravestone. On one level, the film was a self-indulgent pastiche of Deren's 'psychodramas', and were it not for the evocative, at times, abstract, and hyper-cinematic charge, I would be too embarrassed to mention it at all. However, there is a short sequence in this film, which finds myself – the filmmaker/ protagonist/ investigator – recording the wind out of a moving train carriage window. This scene is what I consider to be its saving grace in what I define as an early cinematic 'wind vision'. This sequence, although suffused with a mood of melancholy, differs strikingly from a later film that I made about the Shabtai Zvi (the 17th century false messiah), entitled *Goray 1648*. In the opening scene of this later film, the sound of howling wind (re-sampled from *Der Dybuk*, a Yiddish film from 1937), is ominously overlaid on to an image of an overturned and capsized ship – a bleak image in symbolic testament to the transcendental destruction of messianic intervention. *Missing Meilich's* train sequence with wind recordings, on the other hand, provides a contrasting moment of sensual, impersonal relief from what otherwise is an essentially nostalgic, and melancholic exploration of cultural origins.

I have since come to the murky conclusion that one can explore originary narratives in two ways. The first of which involves a claustrophobic fixation into one's own closed familial and hereditary origins. This sense of the past encapsulates a literal, and linear back and forth relationship to time, and often involves the perturbing effect of discovering psychic contagions inherited from familial and ancestral lines. The second way of exploring origins approaches time spatially – and as Dr. Zephyrah once illuminated for me – as a sideways direction into space. And, although it may indeed incorporate the first sense of going back into familial origins, is nevertheless endowed with the energising effect of a lateral expansion into layers of realities, and psychic dimensions that go far beyond the limitations of linear, familial narratives confined to a particular time and place.

This first dimension of originary narratives was revealed to me in its full-blown capacity when I was an adolescent. Upon the concerned recommendation of my school, I was sent to a psychoanalyst twice a week, who considered my behaviour anti-social and hyperactive. Twice a week I sat in a small and sterile 'therapy' room opposite a cold, silent woman with glassy, vacant eyes. The room was stuffy, and the windows were always shut. The therapist and I sat through long, tense silences throughout the sessions, and occasionally, I would throw a ball at her, or a toy into her lap in frustration, and she would respond with,

'Which Lydia is in the room? The angry Lydia who had no attention from her parents? The angry Lydia who is reprimanding her parents and grandparents?'

After months of enduring these therapy sessions I sat feeling oppressed in the stuffy room, not uttering a word, too weak even to throw a ball at her lap. One summer evening I decided to veer away from the therapist's penetrating gaze, and turned my own to the window, peering outside at the garden. The sun was setting, and there was a golden light cutting through the leaves on the pine trees. After a few moments the sky turned an ominous gray, and the sound of thunder struck the silence of the stuffy room. Neon lightning bolts lit up the sky, and a sudden wind rattled the windowpane whose force smashed the pane of glass into tiny smithereens across the floor. We both sat still for a while in initial shock. I watched as the therapist's face turned from her customary self-assured cold, blank stare, as a gradual expression of fear began to fill her eyes. I seized her momentary paralysis as the apt opportunity to escape, and swiftly climbed through the window, and ran into the eye of the storm with blissful relief.

I recounted this incident to Dr. Lizzie Zephyrah, who illuminated to me with much enthusiasm that I had at that point chosen to leave behind, what she called, the 'closed-corners of the psychic and temporal abyss' which was triggered by the 'first dimension of originary fixations', and had departed into 'the second sphere of origins', signified by the 'rapturous-non-human dimensions of the world.' She described this moment as an instance of a 'divine storm'.

Silent Cinema's Sublime Winds –
'Cosmic winds from beyond the frame'

Voice-over of Dr. Lizzie Zephyrah over glitched-out meadows.

Extraordinarily timed, almost miraculous in tone, the wind ripples through the meadow.

The meadow breathes with vivacious gusto; every blade of grass is suddenly awakened and called into being. A stranger from afar brings with him the whirlwind.

The scene of the wind rippling the meadow functions as a wake up call, as the protagonist's mother sits brooding in melancholic passions. The stranger brings her the wind, blowing her into another state of being. The wind is the living memory that ruptures her sense of self.

The wind is the invisible thread laid bare between two worlds. Behaving like a transpersonal messenger it ruptures personal-familial history, effectively threading these filaments back into the cosmic whole.

Cosmic winds blow into the frame, and into the protagonist's dreams. The child-protagonist/narrator is courageous because of the nocturnal wind. Beckoned by its call, he flows into its source, into an unknown door, across a portal. The wind blows the pine trees at night with a voracity of an unknown nature. Its tone is primordial. The blossoms and pine kernels fall in slow speed, swirling majestically in mid-air. The bed sheets billow while his mother levitates over her bed in the room next door.

Mirror can be described as a 'biopic', or as an impersonal 'auto/biography' of the filmmaker's childhood, wherein the boundaries of dreams, political histories, and trans-generational traumas blur into a fluid stream of images and sounds. The wind is a recurring refrain throughout this film; it comes in fits and starts, slowly taking over the dreaming bodies of the characters on-screen, and the virtual worlds of the spectator. It produces what the filmmaker Jean Epstein calls 'a second nature', a cinematic awakening beyond human subjectified states. The camera homes into subterranean worlds of living, swarming matter, sending ripples into our perceptual terrains, producing an immanent world of poly-sensual delight, exhaled from the cosmic night.

Dalia Neis

Post Vision©
Micronesian Navigation

Dr. Zephyrah and I spent the afternoon in an open meadow below her home, identifying and picking psilocybe semilanceata. The mushrooms were growing in abundance on a patch of damp heather by the Eden River; their nipple tipped heads trembled in the cool equinox breeze. Lizzie beamed when I showed her the densely populated patch of the hallucinogenic fungi, "You are starting to get the gist of what I mean by navigating like a Micronesian mariner; you can now drop your filmmaker guard."

"Drop my filmmaker guard?" I repeated back to her incredulously, habitually warding off any potential challenge to my artistic integrity.

"Yes," replied Dr. Zephyrah, with an air of indifference, "before, you needed a pretext for your curiosity, and now your curiosity is opening up your sensorial antennae. You don't need to point your camera at me as your subject, nor the wind as your object. Artists often use their medium as a protective shield. This can be productive for a while, allowing them to cross their first navigational threshold."

Dr. Zephyrah was fond of drawing equivalences between my filmmaking quest and navigational seafaring. Unlike the modern European navigator, who relies on maps, charts, radio transmissions, digital navigational systems and compasses, the Micronesian mariners (Dr. Zephyrah's preferred navigators), feel their way through their voyage, through a heightened sensory awareness – through attuning themselves to the flows of wave, wind, and the constellation of stars in particular. It was customary for her to congratulate me whenever I strayed from the path of causality, and pragmatism. Something was beginning to loosen within me. I had originally envisioned this film would be an extension of all my previous filmmaking attempts. I would make an experimental film that would sit between an essay and a fictional film. I would evoke the wind through sound and voice. The images would be abstract, opaque, flowing in the direction of the Helm wind sounds. It would stutter from abstraction to recurring film sequences of the Sjöstrom film: frozen stills of Lillian Gish's eyes reflecting the sand storm; the white stallion superimposed on to her face; macro shots of grains of sand whirling in the frame. I had accumulated voice-overs of Dr Zephyrah's spontaneous ruminations on cinematic winds. It would be a good experimental film. But I had no desire to turn on the camera, nor edit the footage.

"But we are making a film. It just doesn't involve a camera." Dr. Zephyrah was reading my thoughts again. I felt encouraged by her words, and continued to pick the mushrooms in silence.

Later that night, Lizzie was drying the mushrooms by the window above the fireplace in her study. As she left them to dry, she sat on the window ledge and began to tell me about her great aunt Beryl, who had witnessed totality on the top of Barden Fell.

Dalia Neis

Post Vision©
The Four Dimensional

The empty frame becomes a canvas
from which the world arrives.
Turn the aperture to infinity –
zoom back into the stark void of the galaxy.

Dimensions of post vision
the aperture clicks to zero.
Freezing into intergalactic memory
you become the zero of things
no memory, no image of a memory
a blank canvas.

You click into perspective
becoming a central point that keeps moving.
Everything is moving, everything is four dimensional
realising you are wind filming wind.

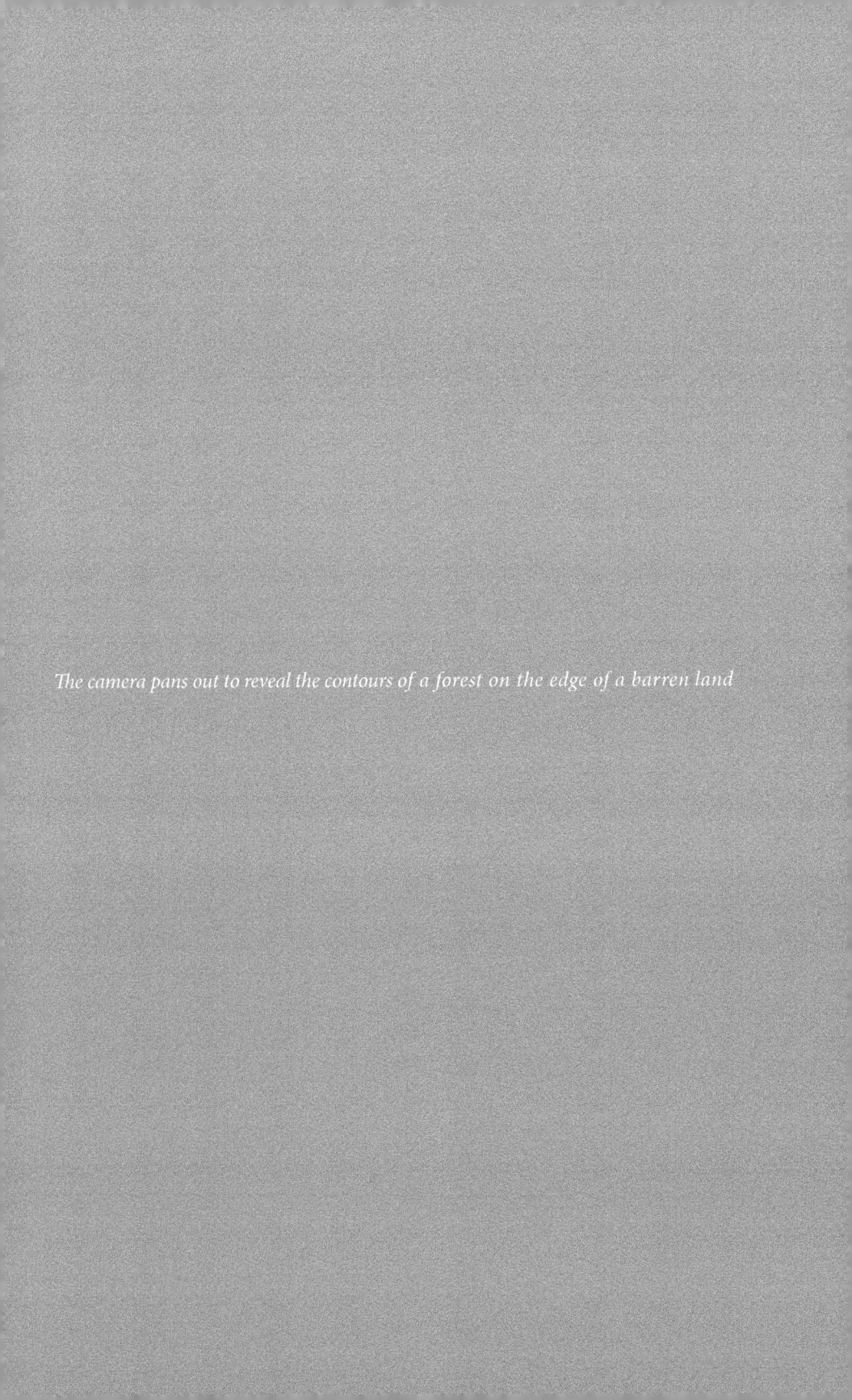

The camera pans out to reveal the contours of a forest on the edge of a barren land

1928 (The Year of Magical Thinking) – Totality

My great aunt Beryl lived in Barden Fell. She never married, and refused all proposals from the young men of the neighbouring villages. Her family grew concerned, for they saw that she had other interests. She traveled extensively throughout the north. She would take long walks in the Eden valley and up the fells; long solitary walks into the sole ancient woodland in the area, which had miraculously evaded the agricultural renaissance. Soon enough, this too was cut down to make room for sheep grazing, and the cattle wandered around aimlessly on the barren, denuded land. Beryl was devastated about the destruction of this woodland, and grew obsessed with discovering the surrounding region of greater Cumberland, its geological roots and history, and she soon acquired an in-depth knowledge of its plant life, stones, former woodland, and winds. Beryl saw the terrain as a palimpsest of former forestland, ocean, volcanic ash, and intergalactic ice ages. By focusing on these layers of time in the present, she began to perceive other zones parallel to the one in which she lived, and became susceptible to tangible, yet invisible frequencies.

As Beryl continued her regular walks through the valley she became acquainted with a young shepherd named Russell, who told her stories about the Helm Wind farther north. He came from Kirby Stephen, a village forming part of the Eden Valley constellation that was exposed to the Helm. At first she would walk towards Kirby Stephen to catch the force of the notorious Helm. She would stand there with her arms wide open facing the northeast direction of Cross Fell. "Take me," she would plead, and soon enough the Helm would shriek down the valley of the east fell side and swoop her up, and she would be carried by it for a while, losing her gravity, delighting in her momentary mode of levitation, until it finally released her with a thud on to the jagged boulders below. After lengthy searches, Beryl's family would discover her, lying face down on the rocks, unconscious and bruised. Beryl's family and neighbours grew suspicious of her behaviour, and by her sudden loss of consciousness each time the Helm wind blew. They were mystified by her solitary walks across the valley of Eden and up the fell. The neighbours would gather and speak:

"That girl isn't led by God."

"She follows the breath of demons."

"They call it Fiend's Fell up there for a reason."

"Only the wife of Satan would go up there."

"Your daughter is a witch."

"How did she suddenly acquire knowledge of the properties of plants?"

"They say that she dances in circles on the top of Fiend's Fell, like the wicked heretic Ann Lee."

Her mother forbade her to walk alone in the hills, and so over a period of about a year she gradually began to fit back into village life. The boys began to woo her again. She was even honoured with the title 'village herbalist', as locals from Barden Fell and beyond began to visit Beryl, seeking guidance and remedies for their ailments. She soon became normalised in the eyes of the villagers. No-one mentioned another word about her being the wife of Satan. But Beryl was on a secret mission; she had heard from Russell, the shepherd, that there would be a total eclipse of the sun in the coming summer. This occurrence would be visible at the crack of dawn. She planned to experience totality on the top of Barden Fell with Russell and his sister Meryl. On the surface, this all seemed like an ordinary venture. The eclipse, after all, was a nationally celebrated event. Thousands would travel from down south up north to witness totality. It was a simple plan. Beryl intuited that this eclipse would break open a passage for her, an escape out of her tedious village life. Both Beryl and Meryl shared a growing religious conviction that totality would bring them salvation. They were not able to explain why, but they both knew that they were right. Meryl would visit Beryl at her village. They would walk to the nearest meadow, making sure they were out of sight from the suspicious villagers. There they would talk animatedly about the eclipse, the wind, and the former forests that haunted their terrain. They often lay down on a patch of soft heather, drawing themselves together, rolling slowly across the mossy ground. Blades of grass, patches of wild flower, flies, and spiders would mesh with the girls' rolling bodies. They soon became lovers, meeting every night as soon as the village lights went out.

Totality left an indelible mark on Beryl and Meryl, opening up their courage for curiosity to explore the world around them, expanding their perceptual terrains. Colours appeared more vivid after the eclipse. They both felt lighter, as if 'gravity had given way', and they would speak of a slight hovering motion that would lift them a fraction off the ground. Meryl would tell Beryl about the ground being lifted under her feet, and her sensation of becoming a body-shaped eye; an eye that roamed through the valleys, an eye that saw panoramically, across the Eden Valley all the way up to the heliosphere. Soon after, Beryl began to have a series of visitations from a forested terrain that existed in a parallel world. Her visions of these forests were transmitted to her through a gale blowing through her bedroom window; the wind would speak to her through hissing spurts of gas-choked gasps, and tell her stories of the former forestland that surrounded Cross Fell, with its sprawling tree-filled nexus at the summit.

The next morning at the crack of dawn, Beryl rode with Meryl on horseback towards the summit of Cross Fell. As they approached the mouth of the fell, the Helm Wind began to blow, but they rode up furiously against the teeth of the wind. Beryl was discovered the next day on the foot of the fell, bruised and unconscious, but all traces of Meryl and the horse had vanished. After Beryl regained consciousness, the villagers took her to court. When the court interrogated her about the incident she told them that she was sent by the Helm Wind to Cross Fell. She was institutionalised for the rest of her life.

"What did happen to Meryl and the horse?" I asked, interrupting this tale.

"Well, there are two possibilities," Dr. Zephyrah continued, "the first, according to general opinion, was that the wind blew them deep into the cracks of the boulders. A second possibility was that they leaped seamlessly across a portal into another dimension. Beryl was possibly not ready to take that leap, but she evidently regretted it. They say she lost her mind. During her time in hospital she discovered the legacy of Ann Lee and read a book about her life. I have that original copy over there on the window ridge next to my plant and stone collection. Although my aunt did not harbour Christian beliefs, nor claim to be a messianic messenger, she persistently practised a version of Ann Lee's circle dance everyday, and later called herself a Shaker. Unlike Ann Lee, who was followed by an entire congregation, I, and only a handful of others, supported her claims. She danced in circles until her death, thirty years ago."

Dalia Neis

Mother Ann Lee

She'd dance to the sound of the leaves blowing in the wind; in the flat moorland across the peaks; jumping and gliding over bogs, twisting like a branch towards the heavens.

The Shakers would twirl like leaves blown in the wind, and spin in circular movements, flapping like a ballerina's frock in the heliosphere.

In the northwest, one could attune oneself to the heliosphere. There was a faltering and lingering cloud formation, a wind ring, known as the Helm Wind. It beckoned Ann Lee to the top of Cross Fell. There she would see the world in perspective; from the heights of the atmosphere, there the wind roared from an unknown, yet near future, the same roar of an express train that would take her people to the ports of the Americas.

Your Claim?

– That the wind spoke to me and told me to go to America where I will practise my creed, that I might freely twirl around in my windblown leaf dance.

Where will you go?

– To the great plains and beyond, where the boys and girls are driven crazy by the divine wind of the North, as we have here in the Northern wind of the Yorkshire moors, but over there, they multiply their inspirations, and are open to being bewitched.

Ann Lee moves though the fields and hovers towards the mouth of Cross Fell

*Anticyclone:
air spinning outward from centres of high air pressure;
flowing clockwise in the Northwest
counter-clockwise in the Southwest.*

*

Zephyrian Spools (An Essay, A Wind)

The Northwest Picturehouse

On this nondescript Valentine's eve, I walked up narrow suburban streets, past endless rows of identical houses and bare-branched trees, to reach the cinema, which sat like a neglected shrine on the precipice of a damp hill. I climbed up the hill like a euphoric pilgrim, breathless and affronted by fierce February weather. Rain, hail, and snow combined, signifying that a saint had crossed these paths, or that the site itself contained a ceremonial connection to a particular time and place; a sacred cinematic gesture, signalled by miraculous weather. A sudden gust of icy wind blew on the back of my neck as I walked into the cinema's dimly lit entrance. Once inside the foyer a draught continued to blow, this time from in between an open crack in the fake marble, checkered floorboards; funnels of wind filaments circulated in alternating directions and speeds, auspiciously opening the pores of my skin to the upcoming dust storm of the Victor Sjöström film. In the brown velvet-carpeted foyer a row of cracked mirrors extended all the way to the mouth of the auditorium, evoking the shabby air of vaudeville sideshows. Aligned squarely opposite to the ticket booth a large bunch of plastic white roses sat in an ornate vase. Warm, neon strobes of light shone on them from above, suffusing the petals with the quality of cinematic artifice, and filling the air with the sweet scent of burnt plastic and popcorn. Above the vase of flowers, sprawled proudly on the peeling patterned wallpaper, hung an original home-made Northwest Picturehouse poster of *The Wind* from 1928. A blown-up, ultra grainy, black and white film-still, depicting Lillian Gish's dark pupils reflecting the dust storm of the Great Plains. A fiery red caption was scribbled below:

> *St. Valentine's treats you to the ultimate film on courtly love! Lillian Gish is ravished by the demon lover of the Great Plains. Across the liminal frontier, dust devils blow through time.*

Further along the vestibule foyer, past a row of glass plinths parading defunct cinema projectors, hung another equally striking, home-produced Northwest

Picturehouse poster from 1975; this time it was Peter Wier's *Picnic at Hanging Rock*: a saturated, technicolour film still of a group of school girls dressed in white Victorian lace, standing by an interface of a colossal rock. Their arms stretched out towards the crevice, while their gazes tilted skywards towards the blazing sun. Twin captions in bold yellow at the bottom of the poster read:

St. Valentine's day 1901! A group of school girls walk into the volcanic rock, ruptured by the spell of hypnagogic winds.

'1901' – I thought out loud, absorbing, and almost continuing the eerie logic of the Northwest Picturehouse posters – '1901', I repeated to myself. At the turn of the century, an analogous Gothic incident took place. Much to the dismay of the intelligentsia, two 'educated' women from Oxford entered an irreversible time slip to the 18th Century at the Temple de L'amour, where they encountered Marie Antoinette and her guards in the gardens of the Petit Trianon during an electric windstorm in Versailles. Nature, it seemed, casts state-altering spells. I then recalled the opening sequence of *Picnic at Hanging Rock*: the oneirisphere was carefully established through the first shot of the great rock, immersed in muffled birdsong, and the abstract low frequency hum of volcanic subterranean storm; a barely audible, perceptible wind track composed of synthetic sounds accompanied the school-girls on their celebratory picnic to the vast unknown.

Here we had a Valentine's cult of another dimension, forming part of a legacy of mysterious disappearances and other-worldly encounters with the organic world. Saint Valentine; the third century patron saint of courtly love, whose life – equally washed out in a misty haze of dubious fog – eluded the church's rigid grasp of sainthood. He was consequently erased from the liturgical list of official saints, and left to roam freely in the unofficial imagination of local mythological frameworks and ritual. The Northwest Picturehouse played a defining role in this myth-making tradition. It certainly did its best to raise the worn-out, tiresome conception of courtly love to a sublime realm.

On Valentine's eve every year at midnight this local cinema projects films about humans engulfed by encounters with the organic world; films that display scenes of human beings having disembodied intercourse with wind, and rocks – and on what better occasion than St Valentine's day, to celebrate these cinematic liaisons?

Inside the auditorium I quickly found an empty seat fourth row to front centre, and squinted to tune into night vision – strange, that there were no lights.

Zephyrian Spools (An Essay, A Wind)

The auditorium slowly filled up. It seemed that there were quite a few solitary film-goers, judging by the gaps in-between seats. Obviously, we were all here to celebrate a Valentine's of another kind, I thought to myself as I slowly sunk into the clarity of nocturnal vision. In this unusually long gap before the film I busied myself with reading the programme notes illuminated by the faint green light of my mobile phone. Rather than conventional notes, it was a collage of quotations, mostly captions from the posters that I had read earlier, formulated into another order.

DISAPPEAR INTO THE CRACKS

Out in the liminal frontier

Into the transparent fold

Watch the girls disappear

I only managed to read a line from each quotation, which formed an anagram of sorts, a puzzle I struggled to solve as the curtain rose. I stuffed the programme notes into my overcoat pocket as the organ began to play to the opening captions of *The Wind*:

> *This is the story of a woman who came into the domains of the wind ...*

Halfway through the film I was overtaken by a deep urge to fall asleep. Initially, I tried to resist this lull, staring defiantly into the screen, watching the nocturnal sand storm beating against the windowpane of the crumbling cottage. Lillian Gish's expression of terror, slowly mutating into curiosity, followed by trance-filled reverence towards the Blue Norther – the northern wind of the southwest frontier – that haunted the lives of the colonial settlers relentlessly. Initial point-of-view shots framed Gish's perspective of the impending dust storm, swiftly followed by the dust storm's point-of-view of her. Fast, furious, seamless shots of both points-of-view, rotated, widened and conflated the subjective states of wind and woman, fusing into an amorphous human/wind perspective, becoming a perspective that is neither wind nor human, but cosmic and sub-molecular. The wind and Gish performed a sublime dance of resistance, courtship, and eventual metamorphosis. I followed these delirious shifts of perspective, dizzied by their endless metamorphic views. My eyelids grew heavy. I let myself go, and quietly surrendered to the silent images of windstorm in the monochrome Prairie landscape. My eyelids were trembling to the rhythm of the spools turning in the projector. The spirals of the cyclone revolved in backward circles of dancing smoke. The film stock in the projector pulsated and gasped, rotating like black suns. I tuned into this peculiar strain of silent cinema spell, drifting into the frames of combusted nitrate, into the heat of the mute sounds of the sand storm. Pure rhythm and gestures of movements. Sounds of elemental frequencies hissed in my ear. The dance of pre-talkie intelligence. Gish's sublime saintly gestures, herself a somnambulist, subliminally spoke to me.

> *These words are like gusts of wind ... They blow in from the desert of seeing ...They are thin branches cracked by a tornado...In their veins is the sap of their pollen.*

Zephyrian Spools (An Essay, A Wind)

These words crept into my inner ear, gently pulling me back into the cinema seat mid-way through the sequence of a white stallion gliding through the sky. We were then inside a trembling hut as Gish peered desperately outside the window. Dark torrents obscured the window panes. Reflections of the vortex danced in her ever widening pupils. We watched her as she opened the door of the hut, hurling herself into the sandstorm. She disappeared into the grains of sand, the scene faded to black, the credits rolled.

Outside in the early hours of the morning the moon was still up, and a cool breeze stirred the air. I had been walking briskly for almost five miles. Behind me walked an elderly, solitary woman whom I recognised from the screening at the Northwest Picturehouse. I slowed down, allowing her to gradually catch up with me. We walked together in silence by the harbor.

The Wind in the Northwest Picturehouse. There was something serendipitous about watching it here on St Valentine's day in northwest England, itself a terrain steeped in wind and weather lore, a wind-blown plateau of peaks and valleys, stormy moors, and swampy bogs, with its fiery eclipsed suns, and its movement of air with singular frequencies.

As I walked alongside this elderly woman towards the harbour, with my coat wrapped tightly around me, the woman's cold dry breath rasped on the nape of my neck as she muttered, "Yes, this silent picture could have been made right over here … or there," she pointed to the darkness, direction North – beyond the hills, past the Lakes, into Cumbria, "We have our wind, a lot of it … "

Before I could get a chance to ask her about the wind, the woman vanished into the liminal zone of the rising, misty dawn. It was as if I had met an oracle, the woman seemed as old as silent cinema itself, and presumably waded through the hills and peaks of the North. What kind of audience is this, if not a weather-ridden one, tuned in as they are to the winds of this terrain – what does it mean to them to see *The Wind*?

Dalia Neis

Memories of a Northern Wind – Prairie Madness

I opened my laptop and conducted a marathon Google search for the Sjöstrom film. I googled 'Wind & Sjöstrom', and got multiple hits. I saw images of Lillian Gish's familiar expression of trance-filled ecstasy. I saw the white transparent horse in the sky blown up to abstract pixilated detail. I saw the blackness of the nocturnal sandstorm. I saw Letty's hut trembling on the prairie. I saw a spectral tornado emerging out of the clouds. I saw destruction everywhere ... earthquakes; hurricanes of the past that swept up villages and cities into oblivion; snapshots of twisters; blogs of amateur wind-chasers; the Hollywood disaster poster for the blockbuster film, *Into the Storm*; weather reports; newspaper headlines of a man in Oklahoma struck down dead by a tornado; a woman in Liverpool struck by lightning; a blog on the relationship between *The Wizard of Oz* and its weather history in Kansas city; a poem by Christina Rossetti; indigenous, Mojave conceptions of wind; Northern Winds; Southwesterlies; Mistrals; Khamsins; Helm Winds. Then ... a summary of the Sjöstrom film. According to standard world-wide-web opinion, the film had two endings. The first, which was the film's original ending, showed a solitary Letty running outside into the eye of the storm. The second, the official Hollywood ending, showed Letty reunited with her husband, ending with their gaze fixed on each other. The producers found the original ending too 'bleak' for a Hollywood picture, and ordered the crew to re-film it. The original ending was claimed to have never been shown publicly, and thought to be lost.

I shut down my laptop, and marched to the window. I puzzled on the Hollywood consensus of the 'happy end': why would a happy end entail marriage between humans, rather than a human's marriage to wind? Wasn't the latter liaison fervently celebrated at the recent Valentine's midnight screening? Throughout the film, Letty is wooed by men, but the wind interrupts any potential romantic developments. Over the course of this film she develops a rich, dynamic, and euphoric relationship with the Blue Norther. Their relationship (admittedly tense at the beginning), develops into a full-blown romantic courtship. Her gaze is constantly fixed on the wind, and hardly on the men around her. In the original

Dorothy Scarborough novel, the author refers to the Blue Norther as her 'demon lover', a relationship described in rich, eroticised detail. A love that is taboo, but considered increasingly common among women of the 'Pioneer generation' in the Southwest Frontier. While their husbands busied themselves with driving out the last of the indigenous inhabitants, while they ploughed the land, and sowed the soil, these women, left to their solitary imaginations, grew intoxicated by the sound of wind. This intoxication, stigmatised as 'prairie madness' – was a 'sickness' prone to pioneer women who resisted settling into frontier life. Instead, as a mode of pioneer resistance, they would weave complex, convoluted tapestries of shape-shifting vortices, depicting the invisible eye of the tornado. The haunting ghost storms of the terrain's indigenous inhabitants would weave their way back into these women's frenetic tapestries, disrupting any possibility of a settled life.

Outside the trees were still. There was no movement. The birds were perched on the birch trees, almost frozen in their positions. I opened the window to get some air. The air was moist, so I ran to the cupboard and took out a large metallic fan, and switching it on to its highest velocity, I remembered that Sjöstrom filmed the sand storm in the Mojave desert with the aid of large aeroplane wind-propellers. I transported myself to the zone of the film, and to the recent midnight cinema screening. I pushed my face right up to the fan's steel face. The air blew furiously. My hair was streaming backwards then forwards. I tried to recall the cinema screening in detail. I tried to recall the film's ending. The air was drying my face as I closed my eyes to concentrate. Then the film came back to me as a series of flashes: the white transparent stallion galloping in the night sky with its mane blown backwards. Lillian Gish's wide-eyed pupils reflecting the dust tornado, her hair blown forwards. Her slight body running out into the darkness towards the dust storm. Grains of sand multiply from the scratched out, worn out film print. The night sky and sand swallowed up into an immanent frame of grainy void, fade to black, the credits roll.

The Helm Wind Speaks

Who am I?
– A sound.
What sound?
– A voice
Whose voice?
– I speak in the name of the Helm Wind.

The North Pennine Chain

The Helm is the only named wind in the British Isles. It is a northeasterly wind, caused by the geological escarpment of Cross Fell, with its steep southwest drop to the Eden Valley below. The meeting of air streams from the east and west coasts spins in frenetic anticlockwise circles, forming a vortex of invincible power, becoming the apex (according to rumours recounted to me by farmers of the east fell side) – of 'eternal originary energy'.

A whirling vortex, known as the 'Helm Cloud' sits on top of Cross Fell's summit. Shortly after, a bar – a parallel rotor cloud – rotates itself some distance above. This bar, known as the 'Helm Bar', manifests itself as either white or black. A 'Black Helm' signifies imminent rain, which generally means that the showers will dissipate the force of the Helm. A 'White Helm' signals that the wind will erupt with a ferocious force for an unspecified amount of time; this force could vary from up to three hours, to three days, or three weeks.

Gathering momentum, like its sister lee-wave-wind of the Alpine mountain range, the Helm swoops down the slopes of the fell, and roars through the isolated villages of Milburn, Dufton, Renswick, Kirby Stephen, Brough, Knock, Ousworth, Kirkby Thore, and Crackenthorpe. The wind's velocity is increased by the steepness of the drop and only a handful of miles away from the Eden valley fell side – in Appleby-in-Westmorland – there is complete calm. The Helm roars like an express train down the Eden valley, relentlessly piercing the meadows, marshland, tumbling cattle, blowing off ram horns, and generally wreaking havoc for agriculture. Its roar is said to drive the animals, birds and human inhabitants out of their minds. But the Helm also energises the inhabitants of the terrain, incarnating stories, myths, and dreamings, providing a dynamic momentum for tuning into the frequencies of the North Pennine Chain.

I stand facing Cross Fell in the distance; its escarpment looming high over the North Pennines. The sky today is clear, and one can see clearly up to the summit. A cloud of hazy mist slowly rises from the peak. From down here in the valley, it looks like a sublime theatrical machine. The invisible elements of air and wind cannot be overlooked in this range, its magnitude and expressive velocity energetically haunt the terrain. I recall my walk up to the summit of Cross Fell last summer. It was a heat wave, and as I clambered up the boulders to the summit's peak, past the radio station's wind-screeched wires of Great Dunn Fell, it felt like I was being zapped into some kind of alchemical funnel composed of metal and air, which in turn sucked me into the nexus of an originary wind zone. Up on Cross Fell it began to hail and snow, a double rainbow appeared a few moments later, extending panoramically across a view of the Eden Valley and the mountains of the Lakes to the southwest, and farther north of the fellside, the Solway Firth and the Southland Uplands. The wind on that afternoon – although not the Helm – blew with a vigour that I had not encountered before. I felt sucked in and blown out simultaneously. The myth that Cross Fell was the home to all 'originary winds' felt like a tangible reality up there on the peak. The summit of the fell, though not formerly a volcano, seemed to possess a force like lava; the earth felt like it was about to explode, or recede into the all encompassing, looming sky. Up there in the summit was a liminal zone, neither sky nor earth, but a sizzling steamy terrain, a magnetic force-field where the insubstantial reigns.

Cont. Scene 4, Autumn Equinox, Cottage in Cumbria

Dr. Lizzie Zephyrah and I are sitting at the edge of a circular marble table. There are two anonymous hard-back manuscripts lying open before us. She brushes her hands over their pages and brings my attention to two passages. She insists that I read the passages together as 'companion pieces'. She asks me to read them in one go, "breathing the words in like images, like elements from the material world, and breathing them out like stars, suns and galaxies." She insists that it would be preferable to conduct this procedure "over one single inhalation/exhalation breath." She orders me to go upstairs to her study facing south to the Eden valley. I am to sit in front of the window view to the valley, and read the passages as instructed. After completing this procedure, she instructs me to watch the view silently and wait.

Passage #1 –
The Wind, Dorothy Scarborough (1925)

The wind was the cause of it all. The sand, too, had a share in it, and human beings were involved, but the wind was the primal force, and but for it the whole series of events would not have happened. It took place in West Texas, years and years ago, before the great ranges had begun to be cut up into farms and ploughed and planted to crops, when there was nothing to break the sweep of the wind across the treeless prairies, when the sand blew in blinding fury across the plains, or lay in mocking waves that never broke on any howsoever distant beach, or piled in mounds that fickle gusts removed almost as soon as they were erected – when for endless miles there seemed nothing but wind and empty, far off sky. But perhaps you do not understand the winds of West Texas. And even if you knew them as they are now, that would mean little, for today they are not as they used to be. Civilization has changed them, has tamed them, as the *vacqueros* and the cowboys changed and gentled the wild horses that roamed the prairies long ago. Civilization has taken from them something of their fiery, elemental force, has humbled their spirit. Man, by building houses here and there upon the plains, by stretching fences, by planting trees, has broken the sweep of the wind – ploughing the land into farms where green things grow has lessened its power to hurl the sand in fury across the wide and empty plains. Man has encroached on the domain of the winds, and gradually, very gradually, is conquering them.

Passage #2 –
'The Sun and the Fish', Virginia Woolf (1928)

All noses were pointing north. All were traveling north. All were thinking of the dawn. As the night wore on the sky which was the object of so many million thoughts, assumed greater substance and prominence than usual. When in the chill early morning we were turned out in the Yorkshire roadside our senses had orientated themselves differently than usual. The consciousness of the whitish soft canopy above us increased in weight as the hours passed. We were no longer in the same relation to people, houses and trees; we were related to the whole world. We were come not to lodge ourselves in the bedroom of an inn; we were come for a few hours of disembodied intercourse with the sky.

Dalia Neis

Ultrasilvam

It was late afternoon during a snow blizzard in Prague. I was walking arm in arm with Lima, from whom I had been inseparable for the past few months. We had fallen for each other after a screening of the *The Wind* in a ram-shackled cinema in Prague's Žižkov district. My peers at film school had informed me about this rare, midnight, 35mm projection at a cinema where you could still smoke inside. I wasn't quite conscious of my intense rapport with this film at the time, nor was I ready on that occasion to face the somnambulist wind trance that would fall upon me on my second viewing of the film a decade later at the Northwest Picturehouse. I remember nothing of the film on this first viewing, except that it made me feel uneasy in my own skin. It felt different watching this film at home on the computer. It hadn't reached me in the same way. Here, from my cinema seat everything felt permeable; the projected film felt contagious.

There was something disconcerting about watching *The Wind* at the start of what would become notorious as the coldest of winters in Prague for twenty years. Seeing this film at this particular time and place felt like an ominous omen heralding the impending winter. I was overcome by a claustrophobic sense that Prague was stuck in the centre of Europe, and therefore prone to brutal winds from every direction. There was no escape from this bordered-up, land-locked city, exposed to years of political occupation. At least this particular Sjöstrom film was set in a frontier zone. For some reason the idea of a frontier caught my attention; there was a sense of an opening, a passage from one place and state to another. The frontier was a leakage, a liminal zone defined by its state of flux and transformation. The frontier; caught between the dogma of human-state-control on the one hand, and by the ephemeral movements and expansive dreamings of its human and nonhuman inhabitants on the other. The frontier; a virtual-real terrain slipping in between the cracks of territorial expansion and control. The frontier zones of where my father was born – *Transylvania* – translated from the Latin as 'On the Other Side of the Woods' was first recorded in medieval manuscripts as *Ultrasilvam*, a Latin synonym for 'Beyond the Forest'. Transylvania's hazy borders fluidly overlapped with the extended range of the

Carpathian Mountains, the Maramures farther northwest, and the Crisana region which bordered Hungary to the south. It was a crossroads of triangular dialects and passages to other cultural histories and dreamings. And Białystok (the town where mother's father was born) bled into the existing and vanished borders of Lithuania, Belarus, and Ukraine – formerly part of East Prussia and a conferred part of the Russian Empire. *Białystok* was translated as 'The White Slope' as a result of its restless and shifting borders. My family escaped from Białystok and the wider region of Galicia through to Siberia which they later referred to as the 'stormy forests of antiquity'.

Victor Sjöström's *The Wind* elicited a memory (that I had not personally experienced), but felt psychically and bodily while sitting in that cinema seat in Prague at that precise moment in time; the blizzard of the cold winters of my family origins, their borderline places and migrations, and the coldest of winters in Prague. The cinema was not heated, which made things feel even icier when confronted by the desert-induced dust storm of the southwest frontier. I compulsively smoked a pack of Marlboro Reds in an effort to warm myself up. Lima was sitting next to me, and although we had not met before, she handed me a silver cantor of whiskey. I accepted it with desperate gratitude and slung it generously down my throat.

Months later, as the blizzard began to die down, Lima and I decided to head towards the Old Jewish Cemetery. We linked arms as we walked through the jagged gravestones while I told her a story about the Maharal of Prague (whose grave we walked past), otherwise known as Rabbi Loew ben Bezalel, whom, upon reciting an amalgamation of the Hebrew letters shem (name) and emet (truth), created a being made of earth that protected the Jewish community from a pogrom. I proudly described to Lima in detail the Maharal's idiosyncratic, kabbalistic practice, which involved dissolving alphabetical letters and words on his tongue before voicing them out loud; and how – through a process of alchemical permutations – the letters became shape-shifting three-dimensional sounds, which paved the way for the existence of four-dimensional life forms.

The sharply crooked contours of the uneven grave stones, coupled with the blizzard and my euphoria from being in the company of Lima, transported me into a feverish zone, and I felt for a moment that I was gracing a stage set of the 1920s German Expressionist film, *Der Golem: Wie in der Welt Kam*. I began to take on the persona and starring role of Rabbi Loew, and proceeded to recite an impromptu incantation:

Dalia Neis

SAVE US FROM GRAVITY

The North-South divide
    Your
defies my side
      Opened
at the sun's last dial
    Mouth
across the feline's tail
      Becomes Undone

אִתְקִימֶע אָרִיבְל אָמָר אָרְגִיאֶם

Rather than making her laugh (a reaction for which I had hoped), my incantation frightened Lima. Taking full advantage of her vulnerability, I pulled her towards me and stopped the recitation. But the blizzard broke out again with furious gusto, interrupting what could have been our first romantic embrace. The graves of the old Chassidim were covered with snow, and the grandeur of the cemetery was concealed in pristine whiteness. We took shelter under the crooked roof of the wooden tower by the caretaker's hut. We sat on a cold bench and gazed into the luminous white abyss before us. I proceeded, urgently and breathlessly, to tell Lima about my curiosity and reasons for coming to Prague; that I had come to take a break from my oppressive religious background, and that I had come not just for the film school, and the cinema history there, but on account of my grandfather's teachers – the seven scholars from Białystok who had escaped to Prague on the back of the wind.

The Haunted Screen

From the vaults of the forgotten archives
cinematic artefacts were destroyed and resurrected
through the memory of her writing in 'The Haunted Screen'
Lotte Eisner breathes life into the ruins of expressionist film.

Ashes to ashes, the concave mirrors
and the translucent interiors of *Lupae*
hovering over collapsible stage sets.

Microscopic particles of fermenting chemical substances
(this is true alchemy), this is the real deal
mutations taking place with a pure fluttering ejection
of lens ammunition.

The last breath of Gothic realism
the poetics of space distorted and unravelled
through the magnification of complex optical systems
– out of the mouth of the golem –

    yud hey vav hey

THE ORIGINARY ALCHEMICAL CODE FOR ALL CREATION

Dalia Neis

Having Sex with the Wind

"Did you sleep with her?" Dr. Zephyrah asked. We were sitting on a branch of fallen birch, gazing towards the stone circle on the outskirts of a damp meadow, far enough out to notice the way Long Meg and Her Daughters were framed at a particular vantage point in relation to the wider terrain of the Eden valley. These Neolithic stones were embedded in a landscape of agricultural domesticity, whose outer edges were surrounded by unkempt marshland, ruined quarries, and defunct industrial drainpipes. Farther off to the distance stood the hills and crags casting a dark shadow on to the evening light.

"I had a blackout … " I replied, "then the next thing I knew, I woke up in her bed. It was in the middle of the night, I woke up with a start, freezing cold. I saw her lying naked next to me. The window was slightly ajar, and let in an icy breeze. I remember getting up, and walking towards the window to close it, then going straight back to sleep."

"You were with Lima in the snow blizzard in the cemetery – then together in bed, but what happened in between?"

Dr. Zephyrah was persistent. I had grown accustomed to her acute interest in my nebulous sex life. At first she had seemed nosey and invasive, but after a while, it occurred to me that it may have formed part of her wider recapitulation process.

"We grew apart after that night," I continued. "I wasn't able to explore anything more with Lima. It was as if we both knew that we had crossed some kind of threshold together, but we were both confused and afraid about the nature of this threshold, whether it was psychic, sexual, or –"

"Had you had other encounters like this before Lima?" Dr. Zephyrah queried.

"Well, yes," I replied. "I seem to have them all the time – these liminal encounters, not knowing which direction they will take, or the precise nature of what they actually are." I was thinking, at that precise moment, about my encounter with Dr. Lizzie Zephyrah, but dared not admit this to her.

"Long Meg and Her Daughters," Dr. Lizzie Zephyrah mused out loud after a long pause, as if deliberately trying to shift my thoughts away from her to the landscape around us, "are stones of no apparent everyday function, yet are endowed with symbolic and historical significance by the local inhabitants. Do we consider them as a coven of witches who were cursed and turned into stones by an angry Lord, or do we perceive them as articles of prehistoric worship?"

"Maybe both," I replied half-heartedly, frustrated with the random shift of conversation topic, but realising too late that she was posing another one of her rhetorical questions.

"Long Meg," continued Dr. Lizzie Zephrah, taking my hand gently, while leading me onto a bracken path towards the largest of the oval stones. "Long Meg is located in the northwest of the British Isles, yet it is also positioned within the wider strata of northwest Europe. The cardinal points of Long Meg are perpendicularly aligned to the northwest, forming an exact polar counterpoint to the southwest. The stone circle itself is surrounded by the outer Cumbrian frontier, and farther North, Cross Fell, then Scotland, out there in the distance … and if you turn around and look towards the southwest –"

We turned around slowly together, silently facing southwest to a view of an exposed, flat meadow.

"In a moment you will see the sun setting on the nape of Long Meg's neck," continued Dr. Lizzie Zephyrah breathlessly, "it will cast an unusual light across the meadow, sparking electrical currents in the atmosphere." She pointed her index finger towards an indefinable point of meadowland in front of me.

A flock of herons glided towards us, and I followed their direction of flight as they swooped north towards Scotland. Then a light westerly wind began to blow, and I turned around to face Dr. Lizzie Zephryah – her hair swept forward across her face, as she stood, head raised high, her eyes fixed on a distant point in the sky. I slowly reached out to take her hand, moving towards her, but grew faint and slowly fell to the ground, as if gravity had suddenly given way. From the corner of my left eye, lying on the ground, I saw Dr. Lizzie Zephyrah parting her legs and raising her skirt slowly to her hips, as if inviting the wind to enter her. I allowed myself to fall back across the damp meadow, folding myself into a ball. I continued to roll, not wishing to stop, feeling a rush from the coolness of the mossy ground on my skin.

Dalia Neis

Seven Scholars

The year was 1928, it was the first day of Elul, and the inhabitants of Białystok were running through the town centre towards the synagogue. There were passing rumours that a band of thugs from the neighbouring towns and villages were on a violent rampage, invading the shtetls, stealing money and gold, looting Jewish homes, libraries, and synagogues. The synagogue's modest hall was filled with families, vagabonds, beggars, and thieves, who were all relieved to be gathered there, temporarily sheltered from the imminent eruption of a pogrom. Their safety wasn't guaranteed, but the inhabitants of Białystok felt comforted by the Holy Ark and the scrolls of the Torah, whose words were brought to life to form spells of defiance and protection. Half-asleep, the Rabbi of Białystok stood in front of the red velvet covering of the Holy Ark, mumbling feverish prayers aloud through his worn-out lips.

The Rabbi's wife Shoshana, and their daughter, Sara, were not among those sharing the collective refuge in the synagogue. They had planned an emergency meeting to be held on the outskirts of Białystok, at the edge of the forest, under the Bartak, an ancient oak tree that dated back more than five thousand years. High above this secret gathering the sky put on a ceremonial spectacle: stars from disparate galaxies collided and enmeshed into clusters of constellations and alien shapes before dispersing and retreating into their archetypal forms. The animated canopy of stars formed a striking counterpart to the group of humans below. An entrancing cinema of moving lights unfolded, a slide show in motion, brimming with primeval messages in the language of eternal efficiency. As the night progressed Cassiopeia the Queen appeared to the northeast, her flattened "W" flickering like a neon strobe against the background of the Milky Way.
Shoshana the Elder stood amongst the women and girls there, abruptly halting the heated discussion with her signature hand motion. Shoshana was a self-professed expert in skylore and astronomy. One could always see her small, scrawny figure perched on the rooftop of her thatched hut, squinting into the night sky with her prized telescope. Addressing the crowd, she raised her voice to speak in her customary stern tone: "We are fortunate tonight to behold a rare glimpse of the

cosmic spectacle above us. Seldom does Cassiopeia the Queen appear so brightly as she has tonight. We have here an occurrence that offers precise counsel about the nature of our terrible situation here in the town of Białystok. Behold, the dead, dying, and newly born stars in the galaxy of Cassiopeia are concealed in a foggy cloud of stellar sand and dust. The galaxy emits an eternal, unfolding wind. The stars caught up in this solar gale have begun to coalesce into a comet that now glides across the mesosphere. These stars are the celestial equivalent of our community in Białystok and signal our collective escape."

The women fell silent as Shoshana spoke, and grew transfixed by her words. They shifted their collective gaze dreamily into the night sky, reading the constellation above them with intrigue and awe. All seven possessed singular strengths, attributes and powers – there was Shoshana the Elder, Tamarah the Talmudist, Devoreleh the Kabbalist, Eleanora the Levitator, Faigle the Wordsmith, Sara the Siren, and finally, youngest of all, there was Lilit the Seer, who harboured oracular and divinatory talents of a telekinetic and telepathic nature. Against the backdrop of the turmoil and the violence in the region, and their perceivably controversial nature of their gatherings, they strove to keep these scholastic, magical, and pragmatic exchanges confidential. No other inhabitant of Białystok could know of their whereabouts, every month at midnight, on the birth of the new moon. And no one from their village would guess what they were concocting during these extended nocturnal meetings.

Standing in a still, silent circle, the group proceeded to rotate slowly. At first in tight spirals, before widening them to match the diameter of the ancient oak tree. They continued to spin around the Bartak faster and faster, not once stopping to catch their breath, not once looking at the sky above them. A fierce northern wind erupted, and the branches and leaves of the tree began to tremor. The group, in the midst of their relentless rotations, seemed oblivious to the thick, black clouds which whirled in the sky, concealing, then exposing, Cassiopeia. The stars turned a pale green, and the serene sound of cosmic storms sang alien refrains as the group slowly levitated into the Białystok sky.

The camera circulates around the Bartak tree before gliding through the valleys towards Prague

Silent Cinema's Sublime Winds –
The Sorceress(es)

Voice-over of Dr. Zephyrah over a collage of semi-obscured 16th century etchings of Sabbath ceremonies and court trials.

The relationship between witchcraft and wind in film harks back to the silent era, and to the infamous portrayals of witches dating back to medieval times. In Victor Sjöström's *The Wind*, there are notable interconnections between the natural world and the construction of femininity through the particular prism of a woman's relationship with a tornado; Lillian Gish's encounter with wind is portrayed as an ecstatic possession. Her bodily gestures and facial expressions harbour an uncanny resemblance to 'witchcraft' etchings from the sixteenth to eighteenth centuries – from the unruly, wind-blown hair of a woman leading a Sabbath ceremony in Jan van de Velde's seventeenth century 'The Sorceress' – to the eighteenth century lithograph of a witch trial in Salem, attributed to the American artist, Joseph Baker, wherein a woman is depicted summoning storm and lightning bolts into the throes of a witch trial in a Massachusetts courtroom.

Dalia Neis

Disembodied Intercourse

I knocked on the door of her study and entered when there was no reply. She was lying asleep on her velvet couch. Her shirt was open, her hair loose and unruly, her breasts exposed to a cool breeze which flowed in from an open window, bringing with it a fresh fragrance of mint and thyme from the garden of herbs outside. Her horn-rimmed glasses were on the floor by the sofa, and a manuscript half-read was sprawled over the edge of a large, glass coffee table. I had never seen her asleep before; there was something thrilling about catching her unawares. She always gave me the impression of being intensely awake and hyper alert. I now had the opportunity to study her face in detail. Without her glasses concealing her face I could see that she had soft features, and that her skin was smooth, with singular laughter lines marking the edge of her eyes. I could never tell her age, though she seemed older than me; but that may have been because she had functioned as some kind of mentor to me, and that I was in the process of learning from her about how to navigate like a 'Micronesian mariner'. She appeared to be an established scholar of some kind, and possessed the certified credentials of a film theorist in her academic field. However, at close range, Dr. Lizzie Zephyrah was more of a polymath than a specialist in one particular, academic discipline. She was a medieval Andalusian scholar, who straddled fluidly: poetry, science, herbalism, philosophy, astronomy, and divination. There was something lightly inquisitive in her tone towards me. She was always curious about the 'intent' behind my decisions and motivations.

"But why are you trying to make this film at all?" She would probe, "Go pick some mushrooms."

While I would protest outwardly and defend my actions, I secretly agreed with her sentiments. I would continue to 'prepare' for the filming through staying at her home, walking with her through the valleys and up the fells, and through studying texts and following her instructions, which she dictated to me during sleeping and waking hours.

But now she was lying before me, fully exposed and unknowing. 'She is beautiful,' I thought to myself, as I fixed my gaze on her face, and slowly panned down her sleeping body. As I stood contemplating her breasts, I felt drawn to moving towards her and was overcome by an urge to jump on the couch and –

"Your libido is very loud," Dr. Zepyhrah suddenly interrupted my thoughts.

My cheeks turned red and began to burn with rage and embarrassment. "What do you mean?"

"You know what I mean," she responded nonchalantly, almost indifferently, as she sat up wrapping a robe around her, "I gave you instructions to have disembodied intercourse with the sky, not with me." She turned to me wide eyed, smiling enigmatically.

" Must I choose between the two?" I replied coyly, calming down a little.

"You need to get to know the sky first."

I turned around and sulkily left her study. I walked outside into the dusk, and slowly climbed up Cross Fell.

Night storms were like a dream
– A sound one?
No, a wet one. A wet dream

centuries return across the hills like fire

Zephyrian Spools (An Essay, A Wind)

The Cardinal Points

Later that night, I was dreaming that Dr. Zephyrah woke me at the crack of dawn to watch a documentary that she had made on wind. I was not surprised to discover that not only was she a kabbalist, and a film scholar, but also, a filmmaker, and other things that I don't yet have names for. I walked through the dimly lit corridors. Dr. Zephyrah's home no longer felt like an intimate, domestic space, but an impersonal, vibrating headquarters for investigations of anomalous winds. Draughts of air from unknown sources and directions erupted sporadically through the cracks in the wooden floorboards. I was walking barefoot, my feet refreshed by every blast of cool air, and by the warmth of the oak wood beneath me. The fusion of heated wood and cold air sent rushing waves of focused energy through my body. As I approached the living room, recognised by the flashing reflections of TV lights, I began to hear laughter emanate from a room that I hadn't known existed. I wasn't aware that Dr. Zephyrah lived with other people, and I was certain that I had explored every crack, corner and cobweb of her home. The laughter continued to resonate through the closed door of a non-existent room. It sounded like the lucid laughter of a woman who was engaging with a cosmic joke of some kind or another. It had a soft ethereal texture, the laughter of a person with whom I could quite easily fall in love.

Just as I was about to inquire about the woman's laughter and the non-existent room, Dr. Zephyrah zapped the TV controls into action. Her eyes lit up as a series of flashing technicoloured animations of forested landscapes, extinct animals, rare stones and strange plants, populated the TV screen. I wasn't expecting Dr. Zephyrah to make an animation, nor one of such technological detail. It had the quality of a pre-historic folk tale, yet it was suffused with colours and forms that came from far-flung, and indeterminable futures. It had associations with Anime, in its fiercely vivid juxtaposition of futuristic vision with primeval ambience, minus the urban technocratic, sci-fi elements. It was technically 'animation', except it felt hyper-real, as if the world there on-screen, and the world here in this living room, began to bleed into each other. My analytical-neurotic need to refer it to other moving image examples came to an abrupt end as a voice-over began to narrate a series of enigmatic instructions over wildly morphing, shifting flute sounds:

There exist compass points to other dimensions
that lead through doorways of higher suspensions
I bequeathed the collection of the 11,000 fragments
in Syriac, Ladino, Hebraic, Aramaic, & Arabic
from the Genizah Synagogue of Ben Ezra in Old Cairo
among the original medieval manuscript of section V
from the Sefer Yetzirah
on the Eve of the Penumbral Eclipse at the John Rylands Library
moments before your first breakthrough
I watched as your skin began to flush
and your eyes swelled
from the spherical powers
and whirlwind intensity
on the spirit-wind of words and matter
summoned by the four cardinal directions
under the time-warp of crystal thinking
and its movement across infinite space
through breath, sound, word
re-entering into the palm of your hand
and the porous map of your lower body
your upper arms and face.

Zephyrian Spools (An Essay, A Wind)

The wind that sweeps its force down the aquamarine forest, feel its force, feel its force! Ice age, dark age, crimson age of delight, the unknown interface of intergalactic (k)nights. The semen of the Tempest spits its force field to the night. From which direction it cometh, neither left nor right, the centre of your might, the zenith of zeniths, the zur of sur, we are the centre of the cardinal points, the eye of the velvet brown throws. Nothing is within or without, nor above, nor below the shape of fire buds drifting in the air, 'Wherein the lay of the land emits stark snuffled sounds, melodies of nigh, the neighbouring wind swirling in the sky.

Dalia Neis

Turn around and spin around and around this land, and shout out the cardinal points till you stop, then continue spinning around, and streamlines spiral out, and you will meet the wind's directions, its force field will feel lighter, rising above the land, until you become a dust blown feather.

*The animated plants, stones, trees, and animals
shimmer and sway in time to the rhythmic
command of the voice.*

*The animals begin to move closer towards me,
their eyes fixed in the distance beyond the frame.*

*Jackals, Deer, Lion, and unrecognisable species from the remote past
align themselves calmly on the rocks and blades of grass.*

*The long-lost voice
of a notorious chasidic cinema saint,
continues.*

Dalia Neis

N

The ecstasy of Northern wind
that reaches into your pores
across the thirteen cardinal points

Breathe in the North point of where you stand
inhale its 'Northernness'
breathe in 'North'
the 'North' of England
the 'North' of the hemisphere
breathe in the Northern wind of Northern England
then, breathe the Blue Norther of the Southwest Frontier.

Silence.
The animals face me
their gazes fix on mine
waiting for me to obey the instructions.

I breathe.
I breathe in 'North'.

The camera pans slowly around the Northwest of England to the Southwest Frontier and back again

Zephyrian Spools (An Essay, A Wind)

Breakfast the next morning seemed at first glance like a perfectly ordinary affair, with bowls of muesli laid out, jam, marmalade, poached eggs, and beans on toast. The espresso machine whistled serenely on the gas stove, and Dr. Lizzie Zephyrah had all the weekend newspapers sprawled out before her on the large oak kitchen table. Except – she was not really reading the papers. Sitting beside her, I saw that a manuscript lay hidden on her lap, and that she was absorbed by its contents. She was so distracted that she seemed almost oblivious to my presence. I was still quite perturbed by my recent dream. Exhausted, I felt as if my body had inhaled all the possible attributes and expressions of North, it felt like I needed to breathe this out.

As this last thought went through my mind, Dr. Zephyrah turned towards me, looking at me intently, as if having read my thoughts, and spoke.

"Well, that is exactly what you'll do today. In a moment, after you've eaten breakfast, we'll breathe out North and inhale South. It's not as complex as you might think." She stroked the manuscript pages on her lap with fondness, before asking me to recount my dream to her in detail.

As I thought about her comment, I began to recount my dream, starting from the point when I was walking through the corridors, hearing an unknown laughter emanating from a non-existent room in the house. Then, as if from an immaculately choreographed dance piece, the kitchen door gently creaked open, and a striking woman with a long, flowing mane of black hair walked in and sat down next to us at the kitchen table.

She smiled and turned towards me, her eyes fixed warmly on mine, her mouth displaying a dispassionate curiosity about me, "Sorry to interrupt."

"Her name is Lillian," Dr. Zephyrah intervened. "This is Lydia," Dr. Zephyrah gestured towards me.

I began to repeat our names out loud, " Lillian, Lizzie, Lydia."

They both laughed. I was struck by Lillians's laughter, recognising it as possessing the same quality as the laughter that I had heard in the dream. I tried to suppress this recognition, struggling to distract myself from these striking connections.

"Where do you come from?" I asked Lillian in a half-hearted way, hoping to shift the conversation into a low-key tone.

Lillian appeared bemused by my question, and turned to Lizzie, who turned to me and imitated my question in a Texan zombie drawl, " Whereeee doo youu cuum frowm?"

We broke into peals of laughter, recognising both the banal nature of my question, and the appropriateness of the zombie tone.

"Lydia has been trying to make a film about the Helm Wind," Lizzie added. "An impossible task of course, but she has approached it with poise and humility, so at least the process has been rewarding. I only wish she would work a little harder in taking a leap – "

"A leap?" I asked, confused. I then paused before posing a more practical question, "A leap to where?"

Before Lizzie had a chance to answer, Lillian interrupted sternly, "Why Lydia, you are hiding behind your own skin. Maybe if you'd unfold yourself, you'd get what Lizzie is trying to say."

I blushed. These women were teasing me, jeering at me for their own amusement. They approached me carefully from either side. Lizzie pressed her thumb firmly on my forehead, rotating it slowly anti-clockwise, and Lillian proceeded to brush the edges of my eyelids with her left index finger, while pulling my left earlobe gently with her right thumb and forefinger. Although taken aback by these sudden physical gestures, they flipped me into another mode, effectively stripping away reactive thoughts from racing through my mind, breaking open instead a contemplative zone of lucid clarity.

'Unfold myself.' I repeated this snippet to myself, feeling soothed by their continued prodding, and strange caresses. I observed the emotions of anger and shame running through the right side of my body like streams of toxic sulphur, while the left side of my body was seized by joyous sensations of another nature, streaming within me like impersonal lava, and circulating through my cells. They were right, I was too rigid and locked inside my own skin. I felt tight. Perhaps this was the cause of my long-term, unresolved skin rash that would continually appear and disappear throughout my life, causing me great anxiety. My skin felt flushed and warmed by these women's physical touch. My body was loosening up; there was a definite lightness to it. I then remembered my dream, and how light I felt as I walked, almost hovering through the corridors, as if gravity had given way. I felt the wood beneath my feet, and the air shooting through the cracks of the floorboards, circulating through my skin. I then thought about Lillian's virtual presence, and the oblique instructions that unfolded in the animation film.

"What is your relationship to each other?" I finally asked, shifting the conversation away from me.

The two women dropped their hands to their sides and fell silent, looking at me for a while.

"We are colleagues, of course", answered Lizzie after a long pause in a deadpan tone. Lillian laughed her ethereal laugh. I blushed.

Dr. Lizzie Zephyrah chimed in with her typically enigmatic tone, "In the late afternoon we will head out with our team to Cross Fell, for a scene for a filmed-ritual consisting of exhaling South in memory of the southwest frontier direction. You'll be pleased to know that we'll finally start the actual process of making your film."

We finished our morning coffee in silence.

The Magic Stone – Winds from the Zone
Shooting script. Draft#7

'*If every wind had its cinematic equivalent, then what would this one be?*' Frances was deep in thought as her gaze drifted to the south side of the Mexican border.

'*This was all Mexico once,*' thought Lillian, as she followed Dorothy and Frances up to the summit of the capsized rock.

Zephyrian Spools (An Essay, A Wind)

Macro Shots of

Filaments of wind blasted swirls
the eroded remnants of the ice age

500 million years old
folded, lifted, laid down

sea and river engulfed by storms
capped by millstone grit

volcanic froth
intruded by Carboniferous fragments

former deserts of windblown sand-dune
Jinn glazed ecstatic night

Cut to

Sandstones of southwest frontiers
swirling embossed storm-scars

the direction of the compass
defunct

flashes of higher times
becoming space of sun

no more trees in this forest
no more time

fields of streamlined energy
forces of outer suns

ruby tongue emerald discs
the disembodied imprints of wind

Ceremonial camera movements.

Fade to Black

Zephyrian Spools (An Essay, A Wind)

Fade in from black

From the base of the Whin Sill in High Cup Nick, rare spring gentian, bird's eye primrose, mountain avens, and teesdale violets tremor in a light westerly breeze.

A solitary bat glides past the frame, leading us to the mouth of an abandoned quarry.

Disused mines form filaments from other worlds, fluidly fusing with wildlife, becoming post-industrial nature reserve; a fantasy for the lone walker, who drifts past the buried metal.

Lydia, Lillian, and Lizzie, wade through deep bogs and giant stalks, stumbling towards the mouth of the quarry.

Before they enter, they turn around to face the lens.

Specks of white dust begin to rain down as they slowly crouch on a shaft of limestone.
The sounds of subsonic winds and bird song send them into deep sleep.
They fall down slowly, sprawled along the flowers, metal and rocks.

Deer and jackal watch them lie together, intertwined, hair entangled,
enfolded in one another's thoughts,
the kissing of mouths, orifices, and eyelids,
and the fluttering of eyelashes,
tongues gently circulating, necks, clitori, fingers,
legs in-between the knees of the other.

Hair enshrouding all our bodies like a veil and as I leapt towards
this triangular erotic world –

The sun rises in the NW as the camera circulates the quarry

Zephyrian Spools (An Essay, A Wind)

Name yourself
the soft bark of a faultless wind
the norther to the southwest
southern spirals
pythagoras's smooth curves
phosphorescent curls
beaming through the
night of seven suns
forsaken sites of severed stones
seven sisters left their town
shafts of air across saturnwoods
never to return
flying inconsistently
inbetween

Dalia Neis

cracks
rough rides on skies below
shafts of air through saturnwoods
the luminous glow
of the Helm
and the prehistoric rock
that illuminates
the screen
echoed in the driver's seat
we ride
across phosphorescence mines
towards the seven stones
to Long Meg
we ride
as pixilated rhyme
while seven scholars intertwine

Zephyrian Spools (An Essay, A Wind)

There behind the velvet curtain
a prehistoric rock
illuminates the screen
alchemy of setting stones
rising sun and seaweed
animated curtains
napote wolves and swinging chairs

Dalia Neis

They say
it's a Minoan ruin
a shrine to the
seven scholars
exiled outcasts
bathed in sudden subtropical
light

CAMERA ON A TRIPOD AT THE SUMMIT OF CROSS FELL

A DOUBLE RAINBOW

The sound of horses before they enter the scene

*LAUGHTER AMIDST A SOUNDSCAPE OF FLUTE, neighing horses AND WIND
THEIR HAIR CREATING CONJOINED PATTERNS OF LUCID STREAMS*

Ten Sephiroth made of nothing, their appearance is the look of lightning, their disappearance have no end. The world is in them as they come and go. They race like the whirlwind and bow before the throne. Ten Sephiroth made of nothing, 22 Foundation Letters, 3 Mothers, 7 Doubles, 12 Simples. The spirit wind in each of them. Ten Sephiroth made of nothing. The first: The Spirit wind of living God. The throne set from the beginning. Blessed the Name of Eternal Life, forever continually. The Voice, and Spiritwind, and Speech. The speech; the Holy Spiritwind; Origin without beginning. End beyond ending. Ten Sephiroth made of nothing. The first: The spirit wind of Living God. The second: Wind from the Spiritwind. The third: Water from the Wind. The fourth: Fire from the Water, and height and depth, and East and West, and North and South

Dalia Neis

we move outside the circle

Zephyrian Spools (An Essay, A Wind)

un-coiling

propelling
us into
another mode

Zephyrian Spools (An Essay, A Wind)

The sun sets in the SW

the camera glides across the Mojave desert

Dalia Neis

Lights

    Flicker

centuries return across the dust filled valley

CHORUS

Zephyrian Spools (An Essay, A Wind)

In 1928 the lid was lifted
the desert blue with burning witches
out of the spooled rotating sun
eclipsed totality
1927
deflation of gravity
1928
the impact
a rupture

1928

'The Sun and the Fish'
sacred vision of waving strobes
semi-transparent pulsating globes
green amber light
contours of concrete lines
vanish in sight
slipping through ocean palms
becoming
solar-infused
worlds of
elemental charms
a glimpse of a cat without a tail
signals the end of an era
the lifting of the silence
the beginning of the séance
Elizabethan women
the rest of them
all of them
lead and follow
the jackals spoke to them
they lead and follow
then answer with clear voices
that resemble wind blown leaves
gusts of speech
from an open barrel

streaming through
with force like fire
shooting out the pressure
of an open lid
in-between dusk and dawn
a second nature emerged
one that erupted
under the skin
of a new technology
nature became intertwined
with technological renderings
of the

divine

wind
became an aesthetic concern
that bounced through the lens of a new technology
refracting itself back
into the luminosity of primordial letters
manuscript pages left breathing in moonlight
letters spiraling into abstraction
becoming suns of other planets
meanwhile
we see other worlds
leaking through
out on the summit of Cross Fell
scenes play out as shimmering vortices
urban visions transformed into forest illusions
the interface became apparent
then rendered transparent

1928

'A Room of One's Own' was writ
under the bus-stop
in Southwark

Zephyrian Spools (An Essay, A Wind)

at three strokes past midnight
in the broadest of daylight
under murky candlelight
I lead a vigil in the old cross and bones cemetery
for all those
who fell out of gravity
we huddle in the courtyard
shadows disquiet
pulsating elevations
from sudden long lost
communication
across the street
illumination
of the void
into the endless bright void of a new language
into the cracks of a new moon
where the somnambulist seers take over

out there
in the garden

arise

fluid memories of a nonhuman nature
a bright rasp of a shape-shifting

wind

I call you
from the left side
of this desecrated earth
from the cemetery of
elizabethan women
from my vacant seat
at the british library
from the right side
of this desecrated earth

from the corner of this lavender bush
from my vacant seat
at the john rylands library
whose pages are marked
with folded index cards
folded back on worlds
refracted words
spiralling pages
of elemental charms
as the invisible crowd
marches seamlessly through
the cemented shroud
through walls, gates and rooftops
stone palaces
crossing over to the other side
I call you
"1928"
the year of magical thinking
the year that cleared ahead a new wave of hearing
through technological error
and psychotropic breakthroughs
from the hashish spell in marseilles
I sat listening to the breeze blowing the lace canopy
looking through the port(al)
of the great plains
"this year will never be the same"
the wind was shot in the mojave desert
under the magical instructions
of
lillian gish, dorothy richardson,
the script writer
frances marion
translated words into screen
under the cinematographic guidance
of the helm
virginia woolf spirited herself
off barden fell

Zephyrian Spools (An Essay, A Wind)

in the north of yorkshire
the north of england
the southwest frontier
the blue norther
the helm
opened a crack
into the future
"1928"
has no real
contour
i am still sliding
now i speak out
into the transparent funnel
into the telephone receiver
across the frontier
i speak through this defunct telephone wire
across the transparent frontier
to 1928
to all the elizabethan women
who crawl out the trunks
of phantom trees
i speak out to the surveillance cameras
hanging as they do
from shooting stars in space
to the futural voices
from the ocean of pixilated memory
out there
sliding

                              out of frame

in 1928 the lid was lifted
the desert blue with burning witches
out of the spooled rotating sun –